THE SLINKY® EFFECT

METAPHORS FOR LEADING INNOVATION AND EXPONENTIAL GROWTH

LAURA LITTLE

Copyright © 2020 Laura Little.

All rights reserved. No part of this book may be reproduced, stored, or transmitted by any means—whether auditory, graphic, mechanical, or electronic—without written permission of both publisher and author, except in the case of brief excerpts used in critical articles and reviews. Unauthorized reproduction of any part of this work is illegal and is punishable by law.

ISBN: 978-1-5136-6610-5

DEDICATION

I wrote *The Slinky® Effect* to empower entrepreneurs and small business owners to rise above the conditions and situations they face every day. I dedicate this book to all entrepreneurs and business leaders who are following their dreams and hope that the words reenergize and inspire you to continue or begin to live lives of abundance and increase your alignment with your purpose by using our six mental faculties: Imagination, Perception, Memory, Intuition, Reason, and Will.

Blessings,
Laura Little

ACKNOWLEDGEMENTS

I acknowledge the influence and pleasure I have had from learning from and being associated with people such as, but not limited to, my mentor Mary Morrissey, and other key people I have had the pleasure to work with and learn from Kirsten Welles, John Boggs, Lou Gerstner, Les Brown, Tab Warlitner, Bo and Carolyn Fulghum, Les Brown, Jim Rohn, Brendon Burchard, and Bob Proctor.

I acknowledge my family, friends, staff, and the supporters of this book for their help in the process of writing and creating it.

I acknowledge my faith for guiding me in my life journey to this point.

Finally, I acknowledge you, the reader, for receiving this book and using it in the most productive way to evoke your vision for a successful business.

CONTENTS

Dedication v
Acknowledgements vii
Foreword xiii

CHAPTER 1: WHO WE ARE TODAY VS. WHO WE WANT TO BE? 1

What is "The Slinky®" Effect 1
Emerge 4
    Emergence of the Idea from Inspiration 4
    Innovation is Not Just a New Idea 5
    Incubation Makes Your Idea a Marketable Product or Service 5
    The Investor Decision to Generate Funding 6
    Implement a Pilot Launch for your Product and/or Business 6
Extend 7
    Define your Business and Product to be as Versatile as a Slinky® 7
    Begin with the End in Mind 8
    Highly Calibrated "Why" Questions 9
    Highly Calibrated "What" Questions 10
    Highly Calibrated "Where" Questions 11
    Highly Calibrated "How" Questions 12
    Highly Calibrated "Who" Questions 13
    Highly Calibrated "When" Questions 14
Expand 15
    Controlled Expansion and Contraction of Your Business 15
    We Get What We Focus on 16

- *Using the Growth Curve Model Principles* 17
- *Break Through our Limiting Beliefs by Acting* 19

Energize 20
- $E=mc^2$ 20
- *Priming Our Attitude to Energize Our Actions* 20
- *Self-Care Brings Vitality To Our Actions and Business* 21

Empower 22
- *Imagination and Creativity* 22
- *Solving Our Clients' Business Needs* 22
- *Karma Applies to Vendors Too* 23

Evolve 23
- *Design Our Evolution Story* 23
- *Theory Based On Science* 24
- *Science of Growing Up* 24
- *Our Choice to Evolve as Adults* 25
- *Business Leaders Evolve in Different Ways* 25
- *Evolve Our Future Vision* 28
- *Relationships* 29
- *Business and Philanthropy* 29
- *Health and Wellness* 30
- *Time and Money Freedom* 31

Evoke 32
- *Evoke Success Qualities* 32
- *Discernment is a Capability* 32
- *Respect is Earned* 33
- *Evoke Resiliency* 33
- *Evoke Flexibility* 34
- *Evoke Abundance* 34

Explore 35
- *Encourage exploration* 35
- *Recap of the Journey* 35
- *Parting Thoughts* 38

CHAPTER 2: EMERGE 41

Design Your Startup or Recovery 41
Emergence of the Idea from Inspiration 43
Innovation is not just an Idea 44
Incubation Makes Your Idea a Marketable Product and Service 52
Emerge Financial Viability through Investment 68
Implement a Pilot Launch of your Product and Business 75

CHAPTER 3: EXTEND 79

Extend the Business Model 79
Highly Calibrated "Why" Questions 80
Highly Calibrated "What" Questions 82
Highly Calibrated "Where" Questions 89
Highly Calibrated "Who" Questions 92
Highly Calibrated "When" Questions 98

CHAPTER 4: EXPAND 101

Controlled Expansion Leveraging Curiosity as our Focus 101
Using Growth Model Principles 114
Expand and breakthrough limiting beliefs 116

CHAPTER 5: ENERGIZE 121

Prime for Growth Not Comfort 121
Vitality Equals Relevance 123
Energize by Sourcing the Right Talent 124
Brainstorming as a Core Competency of Wealth 126
Priming Our Attitude to Energize Our Actions 130
Flipping our perspective 135

CHAPTER 6: EMPOWER 143

Empower Through Understanding 143

Solving our clients' business needs 144
Karma Applied to our Business Relationships 146
Tracking successes 147
Develop New Leaders 148
Burnout is for skeptics 153
Understanding and Leveraging Our Board of Directors 156
Delivering Impact 158
Giving Back to Our Community 160

CHAPTER 7: EVOLVE 163

How We Evolve 163
The Science Behind the Scenes 165
Nature vs. Nurture 169
Evolutionary Choices We Make as an Adult 171
Behavioral Patterns by Leadership Type 173
Applying This to Our Future Vision 175

CHAPTER 8: EVOKE 181

The Law of Vibration and Success 181
Whole System Business Model 181
Discernment Combined with Curiosity 217
Evoke Respect 217
Evoke Resiliency 219
Evoke Flexibility 222
Evoke Abundance 224

CHAPTER 9: EXPLORE 227

Your story of an enduring, vibrant sustainable business 227
Recap of an entrepreneurial journey 231
Parting thoughts to explore 237

Bibliography 239

FOREWORD

As a young boy I eagerly anticipated the days I would get to visit my cousin. I always loved going to his house. He was a year older than I was, and I knew that I would be introduced to either a new toy, amazing story, or cool adventure when we spent time together. One such visit Included an experience I will never forget. It was shortly after Christmas; I was nine years old and our plan was to compare and share the new toys that Santa had brought. After the traditional chit chat, it was time to get down to business. He brought out the first new toy and initially it did not look like much. It was nothing more than a coiled up circular spiral bent piece of flat metal. He took it in his hands and began to pull and release one end while letting the other end sit in his hand. It looked like shuffling poker chips. I asked him, "What's it called?" And he replied, "It's a Slinky®".

My cousin asked me to accompany him to the staircase where he proceeded to teach me how to make the slinky traverse the stairs. It was unlike anything I had ever seen, and it was truly magical. We would carefully place the slinky on the top stair then pull the top up and bend it over, placing it on the second step and letting it fly! The Slinky® would work its way down to the bottom of the stairs all by itself. As it pushed and pulled its way mysteriously down the stairs it was clear to me that there was some kind of physical force at work. What was creating the Slinky's ability to accomplish the objective? I was not sure, but it sure was fun and enjoyable to experience at nine.

It would be another 20 years until the correlation between the physical forces that govern our world and their application to leadership began to make sense to me. Concepts like momentum, frequency, and gravitation apply to leadership as much as to the worldly physics Einstein described so eloquently. It has become a deep passion of mine to study and apply the physical laws of the universe to leadership. When applied properly and in harmony, great results are not only possible, but predictable.

I love the concepts, applications, and principles revealed in the "Slinky® Effect". Pay attention to the wonderful use of metaphors and leadership keys shared. If you are a student of effective leadership then some study in physics and quantum physics is a must. Laura Little does a brilliant job of unpacking some of the most important leadership lessons possible in this material. I found inspiration from the Slinky® at nine years old, and Laura Little brought the inspiration back into my life through effective leadership.

Sincerely,
John Boggs
CEO / Leadership Faculty / Executive Coach
Brave Thinking Institute

CHAPTER ONE

WHO WE ARE TODAY VS. WHO WE WANT TO BE?

What is "The Slinky®" Effect

My favorite toys from childhood were Tinker Toys®, Lincoln Logs®, Etch a Sketch®, Spirograph®, and the Slinky® as they enabled me to create something new every time, I played with them. One of the common threads for all of those toys was that they were always new, fresh, and captured my imagination. We could create something new every time we picked up the toy to play with it. The Slinky® was great as it was not static. It literally sprang to life when I picked it up. I could stretch and change the movement of the Slinky® in a variety of interesting shapes and positions, but when I lost attention or set it down, it returned to its original position, just waiting for the next move. It required patience to master the ability to place it carefully so it would walk down the stairs. It worked better on our wood staircase than the cement steps to our backyard. It hung suspended in midair for just a moment before it was released while being expanded. As you can see the Slinky® captured my imagination.

As I grew older and learned about our spiral universe and our innate pull to growth and expansion, I began to see connections as I collaborated with clients. The unexpanded pre-compressed state began to represent our comfort zone and working with the Slinky® came to represent the untapped potential we can leverage when we act. It stayed with me for my 30-year career working with innovation and I began to further conceptualize the Slinky® as a metaphor for how to effect and affect organizational development and change. I wanted to share the Slinky® as a metaphor for sustainable resilience and motivation in leading social impact and innovation.

I have captured seven metaphors using the Slinky® toy as the unifying thread that guide us to sustainable value creation as business leaders. We will walk through each metaphor in greater detail over the course of the book. The first metaphor is Emerge, so we will look at how we lead the emergence of a new idea, product, or business. Extend is the second metaphor in how we, as leaders, create the business model and determine the strategy to employ in how the systems are organized and aligned to extend our reach as business leaders. Expand is the third metaphor and it explains how we think and where we place our attention. The fourth metaphor is Energize. We will explore how we see it in the actions we take, when they are consistently executed and aligned. The Empower metaphor is focused on how our imagination informs our self-leadership and relationships as leaders in our business and community. Evolve is the sixth metaphor as we understand our unique DNA profile and intentionally identify opportunities to become more, create more, and live our life with purpose. The seventh metaphor Evoke focuses on how we bring out qualities in ourselves, our business products, and services to meet the complexity of today's marketplace. Finally, Explore is the signal we have built in each of the metaphors and like the Slinky® there is a sustainable value in what we have created that will be our legacy.

We each use our business leadership skills in three different aspects, self-leadership to achieve our vision, mission, or purpose in life. We also may adopt the role of a leader of an organization and use our capabilities to align our organization around its vision, mission, and purpose. An organization in this context may be additive to your vocation. Types of organizations include places of worship, community organizations, and our families. Finally, there is the most usual role as the leader of a business entity as we also lead the business in attaining their vision, mission, and purpose. Businesses have a life cycle of stages: Start up, Validate, Prepare to Scale and Refresh, and Reinvent. These metaphors apply to you as an exponential business leader across all four stages of your business entity's life cycle.

Startup Stage - This means that you and your team are focused on creating a blueprint for your business. There needs to be a clear sense of what the business will offer, what it will do, and how it will do it. During this stage, your goals should be proving your user or customer need and solution, having proof of the concept of your product or service, and ultimately a business plan. This is addressed first in Emerge, yet with the principle of keeping the end in mind, you should not just read that chapter and feel confident that you have everything you need. The book is relatively short for such a broad range of concepts so open your mind to the capabilities you will need in other stages of your successful business.

Validate Stage - This means that you and your team are focused on validating the commercial viability and scalability of the business model described in the blueprint. This involves running market trials in which business plan assumptions are tested. This is an iterative process which results in the refinement of the product or services, as well as the business model. Likewise, incubation of the idea is validation and addressed in detail in Emerge so you will need the rest of the book to take it from incubated idea into a viable business.

Prepare to Scale Stage - This means that your business is preparing the conditions needed to grow a validated product/service and business model. During this stage, your goals should be working towards achieving operational stability and enhancing the conditions needed for scaling both externally (customer education, supplier reliability, new distribution networks) or internally (hiring skilled personnel). Extend marks when we start thinking and when we get curious about what it takes to form a strong foundation for a scalable, extensible business.

Refresh and Reinvent Stage – This means that your business has launched and reached a level of stability and you understand the pull to grow that requires you to run your business and constantly reinvent, reinvest, and refresh to meet our dynamic marketplace and create a greater social impact. The remainder of the book is dedicated to these complex and myriad functions and perspectives that help you retain your agility and nimbleness over the ups and downs of the career and life of an entrepreneurial business leader.

Emerge

Emergence of the Idea from Inspiration

Richard James was inspired by an idea after he knocked a prototype spring off a workbench. He worked through the ideation and incubation process for the next year to create the properties he desired. They tested it with neighborhood children and launched a pilot sales event at Gimble's. The process itself has not changed since the Slinky® was created, yet technology and attention can accelerate the timeframe.

Every day we have new ideas. They come to us in a variety of forms, perhaps as a thought from out of the blue, as a nagging whisper, others are a connection between two seemingly disjointed thoughts and now we have a new perspective on the synergy that can be leveraged. The rest come from discontent because we desire a product, service, or app that will help us in some way. The key is in what we do with the idea, specifically how we progress that idea into something that is uniquely our own but that also attracts a customer market.

Innovation is Not Just a New Idea

Emerging in this case may be around crystallization and market validation rather than what we might intrinsically think of as just identifying the cool next big idea. Ideation is a defined process with key components that can be learned and applied to proactively reduce risk and promote successful outcomes. Start with the problem, unmet need we are trying to solve, then understand the quantitative and qualitative research available on this problem or need. Gather customer data to make them the hero of the solution, competition identification, developing the game changing idea, honing the idea into actionable concept, and building the communication strategies. Investing hard dollars in building a prototype of a product without undertaking this step introduces excess risk in the form of time and money. Now that we have identified them, we need to solicit their feedback. The final step is analyzing the findings and refining our idea.

Incubation Makes Your Idea a Marketable Product or Service

Incubation is the next step in the process to emerge with a defined product or service prototype. This consists of four distinct phases. Customer Validation begins with understanding at a detailed description level who our customer is and what problem they are trying to solve. Our idea for a product or service has to align directly to that solution to fulfill their need. It involves future forecasting of the dynamic customer market, honing our customer marketing message, conducting research on target customer identification, defining best means for engagement, determining long-term relationship strategies and nurturing approaches. The second step is Business Validation, which leverages rapid prototyping to hone the product features and implement feedback, design future forecasting of continuous improvement for product therefore soliciting feedback from business leaders on product viability and tweaks needed for a long-term production strategy definition. The third step in incubation is Business Model Validation, which is covered in detail in the next chapter, and finally the fourth step is Market Validation; identifying specific customers in our target market to validate our idea with a pilot market launch.

The Investor Decision to Generate Funding

Organic growth funded by customer revenue may be desired but not always feasible. Yet, investment funding is not for every business. Understanding each type of investment funding is the baseline capability needed, building on that we move into crafting the right pitch for the right funding model. As you tell your story, it helps you to discern whether investment is right for you or if you should bootstrap the funding and skip the investors, based on your financial analysis of the impact of your return and vision. Identifying target investors and building a relationship with them is essential. Some investors do not even look at cold pitches, so it is vital to collaborate with them prior to having a specific idea or venture in mind to a warm the stage. Presenting the pitch deck and handling investor Q&A is an iterative process. We will need to determine if we incorporate their feedback and requirements into our agreement or walk away at each iterative step. This is all a part of enrolling investors in the venture. Eventually we will come to an agreement principle. During this process we will need to be aware of the specific banking principles and requirements that are tied to various funding types and the supporting financial and operational processes that will be required to produce the accountability reporting required by our investor.

Implement a Pilot Launch for your Product and/or Business

Up to this point the business plan only exists on paper, but now that all of the hoops have been jumped through to this point, it is time to implement a pilot launch in the marketplace. Our roll out strategy is finalized. We have defined our test implementation success metrics. We run the pilot launch for a preset period of time and measure the prototype launch effectiveness for ongoing businesses. We determine our spin in or spin out strategy for the product. This is whether we launch the product as a part of our current business or as a standalone business. Based on the pilot results we then define roadmap to product production and formal market entry.

Extend

Define your Business and Product to be as Versatile as a Slinky®

The Slinky® is more than a toy. As recently as 2012 there was a research article in the American Journal of Physics looking at wave motion in Physics and Continuum Mechanics. It was a fully vetted and prototyped product born of solid engineering principles. Therefore, it could be extended. It was not a random flash idea to fit a fad. Those can be very profitable and have launched quite a few businesses and captured quick revenue. Think about Pet Rocks, Furbys, and Google Glass. They made it big yet failed to serve a true need. In a perfect world our discernment would never fail us as business leaders, and we would always know the difference between a product that served a need that is longer lasting.

The plethora of businesses that serve the need for convenience around mealtimes is an example. Delivery services target that need from avoiding shopping through prepackaged meal kits. All of the ingredients and a recipe are provided. Others provide online shopping and home delivery. At least one vendor is solving a second need, preparing the food, by delivering freshly prepared meals. Still others are capturing our love for convenience by delivering meals from our favorite restaurant. Our goal as business leaders is not only to tap into the underlying need as these companies did, but to establish a firm foundation, like Amazon did with book sales, to be able to apply those same foundational principles in a healthy business framework to add products and services as consumer attention and needs evolve. In this chapter we delve more deeply into formulating an extensible business model and framework from our vision.

Begin with the End in Mind

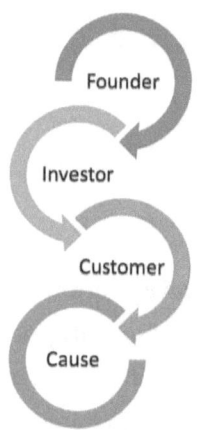

The premise of any business is to drive value. What is unique about the exponential innovational leadership for global impact is that it has four elements instead of two in the value chain. The visual association with the Slinky® is immediately evident in the image of the value chain.

Our leadership mindset is also characterized by distinct behaviors. Our behavior relies solely on our personal experience. This guides us down familiar paths, applying actions that worked for us in situations that we perceive to be similar. When we move out of operating on experience or patterns of behavior by taking a step back and refocusing on the value chain, we allow ourselves to apply new behavior when we know from instinct or research that what we've applied in the past is not an appropriate match to our current situation.

Here in Chapter 1, we identify the categories of questions we will answer before we apply those concepts more deeply in Chapter 3. These are the elements needed when we look to build an extensible business model that creates Value for Me as the owner, Value for the Investor, Value for the Cause, and Value for the Customer. Throughout the book, you will see that the value chain concept and the links are defined by you as you progress through the lifecycle of the business. As with any chain, it is only as strong as its weakest link, so we may allow discomfort for a defined period of time in one link in the chain, but not for an extended period of time.

Highly Calibrated "Why" Questions

We will explore all of the Who, What, Where, How, When and Who questions that hinge on the answers we provide to our Why questions. Once you've defined your purpose and therefore your Why as the most empowering driver for sustaining you throughout the ups and downs, we switch our focus to the questions that are the most empowering for creating the conditions for success.

Vision - You have a full spectrum vision and mission in four dimensions: Business, Health, Relationships, and Time and Money Freedom. The quality of your vision and how it is calibrated with details that create a mental picture drives your ability to achieve the vision. It grounds the series of decisions that are needed and how confident you are in making the decisions in the context of the complexity of running the business while simultaneously reinventing your business. Our answers to each of the other categories of questions emanate from the perspective that this is done, and you are reverse engineering how you arrived, rather than chasing each new shiny object, tool, class, or theory and hoping it provides the key.

Mission – As a social business leader, our mission is our cause, why this business is tied to our cause, how they integrate and provide the synergy for social impact. This should be stated clearly, posted, and become a part of every decision we make, not just a check list item because a business consultant, author, or textbook told us that we need this.

Intention – Each of the above are sweeping views of where we are headed and as great as we all are, we cannot do everything in one day. We set our attention on the next milestone and subsequent action through intention. I chose to begin with the end in mind, therefore, I intend to build a framework that can be extended as our business vision expands and evolves over time is one example of setting an intention. Deciding for each of the following questions completes that intention by directing our attention to the correct actions we can take today. Answering these questions may be iterative, for example you may answer some of the what questions and down the road you are looking at the questions in other categories and realize it is impacted by the answer to a previous question. Modify the original answer and return immediately to the task at hand.

Highly Calibrated "What" Questions

Service/ Product – What service(s) or tangible products do we provide? There is a progression here in thought that will require time. First start with our primary service or product and state exactly what it is. Then move into the value it brings to us as the business owner, the cause we are serving and/or the customer if the customer is not the cause. Repeat that progression for each of our products and services.

Strategy – What is our strategy to offer each product or service? The strategy may vary for each service and/or product. For example, we may offer our services to businesses and our products to consumers or vice versa. Determining how our mission will be best accomplished as a whole is the outcome of this exercise.

Avatar Customer – For each service/product above what is our target customer description? For example, I work with technology businesses to provide services that enable their social impact in the healthcare industry. In the Slinky® Effect this step will be critical in reaching the next step. I do not recommend going broad here if we are a relatively unknown or new business. If we work for a well-established nonprofit or social business and are using this book to improve our internal processes, going broad may work overall, but distinct campaigns for different audiences are still recommended. I believe marketing in general is moving away from the broadcast that send everyone with the same email or the robocall approach and instead building a huge list approach. Setting a smaller target customer audience is better for telling our brand story.

Brand Strategy – What sets our social business apart from competitors? Our niche, our perspective, our product, our experience. Now that we have defined an avatar client, treat them as though they are the lead character in the story we want to tell. What is the one thing our customer wants? We may offer more than one product or service, fantastic, but even Coca Cola does not mix their commercials for Coke, Diet Coke, and other products in one ad. It is not because they do not offer them or because they do not know how, it is because they know better. Focus on one message at a time for clarity.

Highly Calibrated "Where" Questions

These questions require an understanding of our target customer and how they buy what we offer. Do they always buy online? In that case a brick and mortar investment may not be warranted. However, if we are looking at opening a fine dining restaurant, our only alternative to brick and mortar is to offer an in-home chef experience. Once again, it comes down to understanding our target customer and being visible where and when they want to buy.

Location Footprint – What does the footprint of our business require?

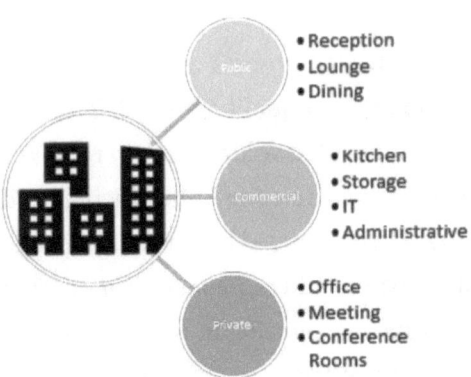

Offline businesses require less funding and presence and are popular for businesses providing services.

As co-working spaces gain traction, they offer a wide range of options for community and options for infrequent meeting spaces and conference room facilities to hold occasional meetings and free up capital to be used for other startup expenses.

Selection Criteria – What criteria will we use to determine the right location for our business? First and foremost are we online and if so, is it a cloud-based business or do we need an IT location? Other dimensions are cost, proximity, and online only.

Location Review – What comes into play? (zoning, permits, leases, licenses, drawings)

Highly Calibrated "How" Questions

For businesspeople, the level of complexity ramps up at this level of question.

Standardization – How will we standardize or customize our services or product? This decision will be based on our vision for how we deliver our unique value to our target customer. Did we answer that we have unlocked the best way to do something? Then we will choose a standardized model that maintains the quality of that unique differentiator. If our answer was that we listen to what is different about each customer and tailor our solution to match their needs, then we will select a highly customized business model. This in turn has an impact on our pricing and anticipated volume. We need to be aware of these impacts as we design our end-to-end process models to be able to oversee the differences that are required.

End-to-End Processes – for a standardized process we can introduce automation and repetition for consistency and quality control. This has the advantage of managing the higher anticipated volume. It may require a higher upfront investment, yet is likely to yield a strong ROI, which should be a metric we can measure. For a highly customized business model, the opposite approach is recommended, we would add more service or product variations and a catalog of the variations and significant investment into the development of all personnel who have client interactions to create a personalized experience. This investment is steady throughout and is reflected in a lower volume higher price per transaction model.

Outsourcing Strategy – for a standardized process business model this is a more viable option. For a high customization business model, a business alliance strategy is preferable. We would create a referral strategy with complimentary high touch businesses that create a network. For example, a hair salon that does not offer nails, massages, or other similar services creates referral partner strategies with a nearby Wellness Center to refer clients for massages, and the nearby nail salon will refer their customers to your business for hair services they don't provide in return.

Digital – for online businesses this is the heart of our business. For other business models it may be a component.

Metrics – success requires measurement for accountability. Financials, customer service, inventory, sales calls, conversions are obvious quantitative measures. It is also important to honor the technical expert in us to measure the qualitative measures as well.

Highly Calibrated "Who" Questions

Growth, whether in the launch, going concern, or scaling stage of maturity requires a review of our organization's capacity and capabilities.

Governance Structure – this structure is put in place frequently only at company inception. Then reactive corrections are made after a growth spurt or new product introduction or decline. Agile leaders connect the impacts of these and other business events and triggers to define the best governance for the impact.

Customer Communications – in the current connected environment customers comment on a variety of social media platforms. They rate our performance, provide reviews, and even new product and service recommendations. It can be a full-time position to monitor all the various platforms, respond in near-time and then also take a step back to review the highlighted information and look at trends and reactions to continuously update our product and/or business model.

Organization Design – For solopreneurs, we may think we can bypass this; however, we must find a way to measure our capacity and have a futurist point of view as to how we will scale without turning to burnout. Other small companies need to look at retention and career path opportunities to retain top talent and to reduce the negative impacts of attrition and turnover.

Decision Authority – For solopreneurs this could be permissions, when do we not act because we do not feel capable of making a major decision. By setting and documenting standards, we determine when we consult with our CPA, Tax Strategist. This step is often overlooked and leads to second guessing down the road. For the CEO, setting levels of decision authority tied to each position in the organization design can incorporate these responsibilities into job descriptions, performance evaluations, and all aspects of their HR policies and procedures. Once documented, it is easier to communicate and proceed with confidence in managing our staff.

Talent Capabilities – this requires both introspection for solopreneurs and an understanding of the marketplace for the talent we require. Defining our avatar employee for each staff role, business partner, consultant, or advisor creates advantages. We can attract the right employees by effectively screening candidates based on their fit to our description. We can communicate more effectively to our network and recruiters, who can be great sources for talent.

Training and Development - investing in our staff is a sign of respect. We demonstrate that we are invested in our own growth and theirs. Each person on our team has the same pull to growth that we do so it is important to honor that by providing the support for their development.

Highly Calibrated "When" Questions

Not every product or service launched is a Slinky® that endures for decades. Some are filling a need because of a trend, fad, etc. Others are replaced by the next best thing. In the 1970's VCRs were the hot product. In the 1980s CDs were introduced and lasted a bit longer, but now everything is transmitted by digital and cloud solutions. Those may pass too. In fact, you may have that next big idea and looking to this book to structure your business model can help bring it to the market.

Extend viability - The power and responsibility were evident in the number of questions and answers needed to create an extensible business model. Extending viability through initiative-taking decisions is iterative. Continue to ask these same questions on a monthly basis. As we answer them, we will remove the urgency that came with answering them for the first time and take a strategic perspective by conducting an analysis on market conditions and other forces that may influence a variation or extension of our initial decision.

Extend our reach - Continuing in the strategic thinking vein, provide a structure beyond a suggestion box approach, which can seem random to staff, business partners, and customers. Remain curious. Ask yourself how your product or service can become better. Establish a feedback loop to gather not only those ideas but new ideas. Focus on the timing or when to implement the idea, sometimes frontline staff have the best feel for the timing as to when the customer's need is greatest, so you are focused on when you can afford it. Sometimes you need to find a way to afford it when the customer needs it, or the moment will pass, and they will find it at your competitor's.

Expand

Controlled Expansion and Contraction of Your Business

We can all visualize the Slinky®. Now that we have the image of the Slinky® in our mind's eye, expand it in our mind for a moment, straight up and down. This is our spine. Now move the image we created, think about reaching for something on a shelf, bending to pick up something on the floor, turning to the right or left, this is our spine at work, supporting our movement and growth over our lifetime.

We know that the spine can grow and expand, we see it every day as we experience growth from infancy to adulthood. Growth is a constant calling as much a part of our spiritual essence as our DNA and as fundamental to the core of who we are as our spine is to our body. As innovation business leaders striving to make a global impact, everything we want is, by definition, outside our comfort zone. This truth applies regardless of what dimension we are seeking to expand. We need to flex our spine and stretch in new ways that may cause temporary discomfort in the interest of long-term growth.

We Get What We Focus on

As Dr. Joe Dispenza says it in his book "Breaking The Habit of Being Yourself", we have the ability to 'fire and wire' new brain patterns that support new ways of thinking and shortcut the longer therapeutic models of rehashing the past and coming to terms with it before moving on. In this approach, we cut straight to focusing our attention on the desired new state and designing the new neuronal pathways that reinforce the new thinking that creates the desired result.

Here is an example of how that played out in the short run at the new job, I mentioned earlier. My first client was a large water system that was ready to terminate their contract with my new employer if a quick turnaround could not be made on their project. To prevent that from happening, I took the following actions in the first six weeks: I listened to my new client, understood their issues, put a new plan in place. We renegotiated our contract, a change that dropped some products that were not a good fit. We completed one of six projects in their program and set go-live dates that were reasonable for the remaining five projects. I had to change some of the project managers on my team, add new team members, and address performance issues jointly with their project management leads on their side as well. None of this was effortless, but it was easy, because we developed a new way of thinking and working together and believing in the eventual success of the project because of the new attention on quantum thinking versus common hour thinking.

In an ideal world, that would be the end of the story. The entire leadership team of 12 executives recognizes the difference in pulling together for a common goal, seeing the difference that this new approach makes, and adopts it organization wide not only for this project, but across the board. Sadly, within six months, the CEO was removed by the Board and new challenges arose and we'll see other examples of how resistance and the comfort zone come back when dealing with large organizations and well-entrenched neuronal pathways of organizational behaviors and cultures. "The Slinky® Effect" does have a limited ongoing motion effect; however for a truly "Unshackled" business model, I recommend, once we have stabilized a solid foundation, we then begin to work with Aaron Young and his program to enhance our business with that capability.

Using the Growth Curve Model Principles

Static situations are the result of operating in a mental pattern. How do we know if we are genuinely thinking or just running a mental pattern? The easiest way that I have found is only being able to identify two options. When we fall into either/or behaviors, we have either overtly or inadvertently closed our minds to other possibilities. One way we fall into assigning only two options is when we allow our emotions to have a strong voice. We assign a good or bad to the situation, the options or both. Then we create this mental box.

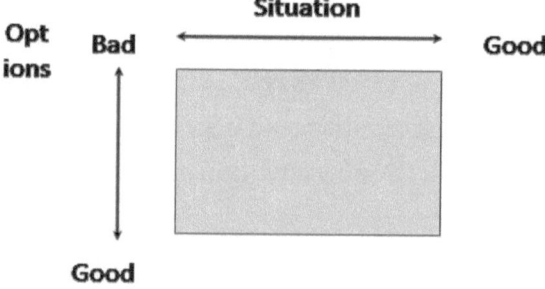

When we assign a good or bad emotional reaction, we often assign good to the current state or normal, simply because it is known. Then the correlation is that anything that presents a deviation from the current state is inherently bad. We may have a steady state business, which we feel is good, therefore we fall into a pattern that defines our perspective and we give excess weight to the perceived bad outcomes or actions.

When we see multiple options for action, we are poised for growth. We look past the anxiety of new and use our discomfort with ordinary to chart a path to growth. Choosing which option, we will act on comes from understanding what area is causing the discontent and what option provides the biggest benefit to address it. Curiosity provokes a variety of introspective questions we can ask to clarify. For example, some may be: What areas are we content to leave unexpanded for now? Are there areas we are willing to take a step back or feel temporary constraint for the overall good of growth? Let us look at an example from my life. I had a great position at a great company; however, I saw an email from a recruiter that grabbed my attention. It had compelling elements, a higher-level position, it was with a gold partner firm that I knew and trusted from my current employer, and the role would help me grow but it was in an industry that I already knew well. I took a leap of faith and submitted my resume. The interview process was rigorous, but I was offered the position. I submitted my resignation to my current employer and never looked back.

Now we will relate this to a social business. We have a day-to-day routine and a framework for running our business today. For better or worse, we have results. We may be in launch mode where we are focused on defining our mission, values, cause, and chief donors and sponsors for the cause. We may be adding organization structure processes, services, technology, and security. The third type of readers are moving to scale a global impact. The themes and principles apply regardless of what growth stage we are in, the details vary as well as the examples and complexity. The first example, that of a change in career direction, relates well to a launch organization. The transition from one path to another is both thrilling and daunting. We have established a history of success and a set of behaviors, thought processes, knowledge, and habits that served us well and became our comfort zone. Throughout the book, there will be examples that each type of reader can relate to since I have walked in your shoes at some point over the past 20 plus years or one of my clients has been there.

Break Through our Limiting Beliefs by Acting

We encourage that pull to growth in our formative years, then subtly, if we are not careful, we shift into other behaviors and create patterns of beliefs. Those patterns can still encourage growth and dreams, while others can become set in stone. For years yoga has been known as a great modality for developing physical flexibility and maintaining that flexibility over time. This is an example of an enabling paradigm we can adopt. It is good for the spine.

Motion is not action. Busy is not necessarily productive. Actions are calculated to advance towards a goal that meets a milestone in achieving a dream. Working backwards from our dream or vision is the best way to navigate the difference between motion and action. Our dream for the business may be to generate 30% EBITDA every month. Then a milestone is generating 10% more sales while reducing Cost of Goods Sold by 10%. One goal for sales may be retain 25% more customers.

This also has the benefit of reducing Cost of Sales. Another goal may be to reduce work by integrating our customer relationship management system with our financial management system. This only impacts the reduction of costs. Actions needed are seeding customer conversations with ideas on how other products and services can meet their needs. Taking time to solicit their needs through online quizzes, surveys, and focus group participation in exchange for a nominal free or discounted product or service. Acting would mean building a spreadsheet to analyze the impacts, answering emails on nonrelated topics, scheduling our own meetings, meeting with unsolicited new vendors.

Energize

$E=mc^2$

To me the Slinky® is an elegantly simple illustration of the principle from physics that a body at rest remains at rest and a body in notion remains in motion. The toy is a simple spring, with the unique attribute that the spring in its natural resting state has all the coils touching one another,... It is what is called a pretensioned spring," If we just leave it sitting on a desk on its side it'll actually be fully compressed." This metaphor focuses on the body, actions, and intentional movement. We start each day with an intention, we can set an intention to achieve or we can set an intention to have today be the same as yesterday. We choose how we turn our kinetic energy into the mass of accomplishment.

Priming Our Attitude to Energize Our Actions

A common complaint among entrepreneurs and within businesses across America is "I am tired". If we begin and end each day with that thought foremost in our mind, it causes us to feel tired. When we constantly think and speak messages that we are tired, we are reinforcing the kinetic energy we possess into the mass of fatigue, weight, and drag. Priming our thoughts for success and energy translates into motion and in business terms, action. One class of actions we can do periodically throughout the day is prime our attitude for success. Starting chronologically with the beginning of the day consider adopting these rituals. Stay in bed for five minutes after the alarm goes off and form a mental picture of our ideal day. As we are going through our morning routine, look at post-it notes that encourage successful outcomes. Take 15 – 30 minutes for meditation to center our energy and calm our mind. Get up and move throughout the day. It is easy to stay chained to the laptop to keep the actions flowing. When we notice that our attention is wavering, there is too much noise, or we need a snack or meal, stay away from the laptop until you have finished the food at a minimum. At the end of the day, review, without emotion, what we accomplished and set our intentions for a good tomorrow.

Self-Care Brings Vitality To Our Actions and Business

Promoting health and wellness, like all leadership principles, begins with ourselves and modeling the behaviors we want others to adopt. Yet, it is more, it is creating the environment where health and wellness are accessible and valued as part of our business model. In the chapter we will explore ideas and actions that can be taken to realize this so we can reap the benefits of increased energy on a larger scale.

Time away from the thoughts and actions of your business can also energize both your business and vision for the other dimensions of your life. If we constantly push relationships, health, and time to the end of our to-do list, we cannot gain the perspective needed. By spending time away, we change the focus of our attention away from leading the business and place it on other aspects of a full life. Our relationships will benefit by shutting down earlier to spend time with someone we value. Our health and wellness benefits by changing the stress levels and workload. We honor our dreams for growth dreams by considering nonwork dreams like travel, hunting for our dream home, golf, tennis, fishing, hunting, and a plethora of activities that we can spend time doing out of the office therefore encouraging us to connect with new people and new experiences that will bring new perspectives.

Empower

Imagination and Creativity

For me, the Slinky® was about empowering my imagination and creativity. It was a toy I could play with when I was alone because I could still have fun creating new shapes and configurations, watching how it reacted when I dropped it from my desk while doing homework. But it also could be played with a friend. We could expand it and extend it even further than just the span of my reach and we would spur each other to think of new ways to get it to move, fly, or something else. We can see that often the most successful leaders in innovation know how to empower others to achieve an objective.

Solving Our Clients' Business Needs

The direct path to abundance is to honor the Law of Compensation. Our compensation is in direct proportion to these three factors The need for what we do, our ability to do it, and the difficulty in replacing us. As a business leader if we understand and solve our customers business needs, we have taken care of both of the first two components of the Law. The next part is in also in our control, to establish a relationship versus a transaction with our customer to understand how their needs grow, evolve, and change over time so that we can make sure we are hard to replace.

Karma Applies to Vendors Too

We can fall into the trap of looking at vendors only in the context of the product or service they provide. The desired outcome for this perspective is to identify the vendors that can become strategic partners rather than solely filling a transactional need. An example may be a supplier of a key component of our product design. Rather than limiting the contractual relationship to a series of legal terms and SLAs that are designed to ensure that we always have this component in stock, there is a way to enroll them in the success of the business through leveraging other products, services, and capabilities that the vendor offers. Exploring this type of thinking can accelerate the power of the relationship. If they have a larger role and are invested in our success, they naturally provide superior service because their success is tied to our success.

Evolve

Design Our Evolution Story

We know that the Slinky® evolved over time. It started out as a silver model and evolved into different colors, materials, and even shapes such as the Slinky Dog®. What is inspiring to me about this is that not all of the ideas came from within their company. They took the time to read the letters from their customers. As business leaders we hope to infuse those same principles into the products and services that form the foundation of our businesses. The way we accomplish how that is done is explored in separate chapters in the book. In this chapter we look at how we can evolve as business leaders. We are not predestined to be business leaders, we evolved into that position just as the Slinky® evolved through our intention, inspiration, and feedback of our relationships. Let us explore that journey.

Theory Based On Science

We generally understand DNA is most typically represented by a helix. This symbolizes the core of who we are as a unique 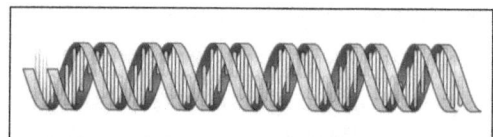 being in this human experience. Even if we are a twin, sometimes we are fraternal not identical twins and have unique DNA components. Through modern science, we know that cells reproduce and regenerate every day.

Through epigenetics we are learning that there is a much stronger connection between health, wellness, nutrition, and success. Through quantum physics, quantum mechanics, and neuroscience, we are learning that there is a connection between the thoughts we think every day and the connections we make in our brain synapses. The observer effect has an impact not only on our own DNA and its ability to change our own brain synapses and repattern our brains and literally change our minds, it also has an energetic signature that impacts the laws of vibration and attraction in our overall universe.

Science of Growing Up

Our brains change in how we progress between birth and 5 years old, 5 – 8 years old, and 8 – 12 years old. Past 12 or 13 years of age we typically operate in the same frequency. Stress and anxiety are triggers from earlier ages when our survival was threatened sending us into the highest-level frequencies. Our diet, family structure, neighborhood, education, and other cultural influences impact our very DNA as part of the nurture effect. This is when our core values are formed, and we see rapid development of both the intellectual conscious mind and the subconscious mind. We experience the world through our five senses, if we are lucky, sight, hearing, smell, taste, and touch. We also develop our six mental faculties: Will, Reason, Perception, Intuition, Imagination and Memory.

Our Choice to Evolve as Adults

We have increasing control over our environment, diet, and other important factors. We also have formed mental patterns of thought. Many of these patterns of thought are beneficial and serve us well. Look both directions before pulling out in traffic, balance our checkbook, brush our teeth frequently. Others serve us well as we achieve a goal of walking 30 minutes per day, reading a book every month, counting calories. However, to achieve breakthrough success in business or in life, these thought patterns (paradigms, limiting beliefs) need to be challenged, discarded, and replaced with new thinking.

This is where "The Slinky® Effect" can help. By translating an abstract concept such as a DNA helix, brain waves, epigenetics, neuroscience, and quantum physics into a tangible object such as a Slinky® toy, it is easier to visualize the cause and effect and the power of decision and action at work when we apply our imagination to creating the business vision that fits our unique DNA.

Business Leaders Evolve in Different Ways

Each of us bring our DNA profile to our social business. We have a mix of leadership types that come with capabilities and skills we can hone and develop. We generally have an area where we are naturally more comfortable or dominant and some of us have developed through experience and training the other capabilities. What I often see is a disparity in how these types are blended within each individual leader. When we work as an employee, we choose and grow into roles that fit our unique DNA, unless we choose to be unhappy.

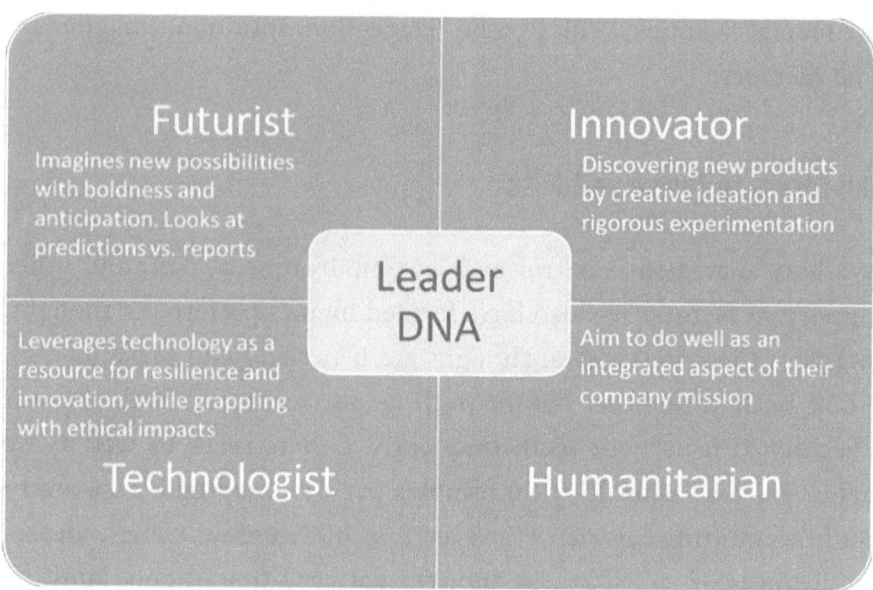

Futurist type leaders see forecasting in context with geopolitical, cultural, and predictive perspectives rather than extrapolating data from current history as a model for what is next.

Innovators take a new idea and then creatively apply the science and art of ideation to flesh out the idea into an actionable concept.

Humanitarians will tend to see their business in the context of how it can influence the cause and make an impact. It is about the mission, the vision, and collaborating with other people who share a similar mission and vision to magnify the impact. We are natural networkers and connectors. When meeting people, our first thought and intention is how can we work together to find a common thread that will benefit each other's common goals.

Those business leaders that are dominant in this area understand that without building a following around the cause and a team, there is no mission. Even if they are a solo enterprise, they naturally establish partnership alliances and business relationships with vendors and providers to enlist them in the success of their venture. They understand the relationship between the mission and the business of the mission and the importance of getting to result and demonstrating value.

Technologists understand how to deliver the best possible solution and constantly strive for continuous improvement. They want to get better, do better, innovate and research the next best way to deliver the best service or product to their customer. They read the trade journals, get advanced training, and soak up any new knowledge out there in their downtime. They are constantly striving to be their best self so they can bring their best to each situation every day in every way.

Wow, who would not want to be anyone one of these personality types, right? Yet life is about balancing contrast and so is running a business. Here is where the other side of each of these personality types can entail and which must be effectively controlled by the other aspects of our personality or our closest relationships to be successful.

Futurist leaders can lose track of details and stick to the high-level vision. They do not like accountability and sometimes are so focused on tomorrow that today does not get paid for in hard dollars. Sometimes they get distracted with the next shiny object or vision and the original vision or mission loses its luster when it comes to doing the work.

Innovators can get lost in the rigor of the ideation process and lose sight of the need to move on to development of the product or service, evaluating it, and then preparing for market launch. A few want to wait for perfection in their minds. The marketplace continually reminds us that customers buy in our current times based on a filled need and they don't want to wait months, weeks, or even days for what the company sees as perfect, if they have a burning need to solve their problem today.

Technologists can succumb to overlooking the power of service in their quest for the right product. This can mean that they do not delegate because the knowledge is all in their head and not down on paper or they feel that training others results in a loss of their prestige or power.

Humanists can be dangerous leaders discarding people, ideas, processes, and systems that are not fully aligned with the mission. They can take part of the organization off course if they are not the CEO. Sometimes, they can be so focused on results and schedules that critical technical errors are ignored for the desire for expediency. If a leader does not fully communicate their vision or the overall leader's vision, there are organizational breakdowns that cause cultural misalignment and inefficiencies.

My guess is that we recognized ourselves in some of these examples at one time or another as well. The good news is that through this approach, we build fluidity and efficacy in moving between these capabilities and recognizing when it is time to leverage attributes from another DNA profile to enable us to evolve. We can do this in a variety of ways, such as: add resources to our team, read books like this one or take courses for professional development, or find a coach or a mentor to build the capabilities of other leadership types to balance out the negative side of our dominant style. Each of these has merit at the right time and place to round out the gaps and smooth the edges in our unique DNA profile that raises our efficacy and therefore impact.

Now that we understand our DNA profile, we will see that it informs our vision and the delta between where we are today and where we want to be.

Evolve Our Future Vision

While we have a capacity for growth, we do not have to be limited to our default capabilities and live a life of unexpanded potential. We can apply the Slinky® Effect to our lives to control growth and live a life by design. We have four dimensions if we want a full spectrum life and vision. My mentor, Mary Morrissey, introduced me to the concept of four dimensions, Love/Relationships; Business/Philanthropy; Health/Wellness; Time/Money Freedom. I have interwoven them with the DNA and Slinky® Effect concepts.

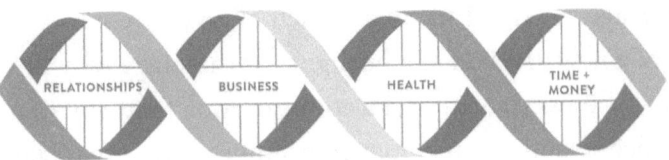

Image developed for New Paradigm Shift by DaniLou Illustrates 2018

Relationships

The social business is built, more than any other business, on relationships. Let us explore them by categories. First, we must have a strong relationship with the beneficiary of our social business, the cause, in order to create an impact with our cause, or we can just be another donor for them. Other business relationships are also critical to build our business. We will need to build a financial model that will fund the cause and the administrative costs of running the operation. Next are supportive relationships. These are outside of the business, they support us just for being ourselves, regardless of the success or if it is a social business or not. Significant others, family, extended family, friends. What is the quality of the relationships we have today and how do we see ourselves evolving to become the person we want to be?

This is where we can apply the observer effect. When we get to the elements of Organization, Customers, Brand, and Culture, carefully consider the types of relationships and the structure of support we will need to implement to create the types of successful relationships that drive a robust social business. We use applied imagination to create the relationship structure we desire. We are the product of the five people we spend the most time with, so choose wisely.

Business and Philanthropy

For a social business these are, by definition, interwoven. These will vary most by the stage of life our business is at. First, we will look at

Launch stage. By this I mean a launch of an entire new venture, not a launch of a new division of a business. At this stage we will be defining the right business structures, location, location footprint (if not virtual), governance structure, customer communications, organization design, decision authority, talent capabilities and training, and development.

If you are some who leads a business that has just completed its first year or two, and you are looking to take the business to the next level, first review the previous list and close any gaps that were overlooked at our launch or, if has been awhile, determine if the original structure can support our new direction and growth without introducing unnecessary risk.

If we are looking to scale our business, then we will be focusing on structural issues from a different perspective. Does the corporate structure support investment growth (LLC need to switch to C or B Corp), IT systems support scalability, organization to support global customer support and business, and marketing plans to scale to fit global reach.

Health and Wellness

The foundation of a successful business is the energy to execute it. Regardless of any current physical ailments or setbacks we may be experiencing there are new modalities and research every day in all areas that generate new knowledge and opportunities for greater freedom and capabilities in this area.

How does our social business tie to our view of health and wellness? Social businesses can have an intrinsic tie to health and wellness. Recovering from a natural disaster is all about the health and wellness of the affected community. Connecting them with the essentials of clean water, safe shelter, nutritious food, and warm clothes are essential for the affected community(ties). Yet, it cannot be overlooked for our organization. We cannot give what we do not possess and demonstrably value ourselves. Our staff and volunteers must be taken care of as well.

Other social businesses focus directly on cures for disease or access to benefits. It is critical to relate to and integrate those modalities into each aspect of our value chain. Publix integrates their care and concern for people with autism and down syndrome by integrating them into their work force. Some consulting firms care about helping social businesses succeed so they focus on only accepting social businesses as their clients, Toms cares about people having shoes, so they give a portion of their proceeds to people who do not have shoes. Bombas does the same model for socks.

This is different than every company issuing a statement like Black Lives Matter after a national incident and then moving on with business as usual. The point is to integrate and be congruent with your actions to create a powerful testimonial and references with authentic brand stories that resonate because it is not just hype or push marketing, it is a part of who we are and our life story.

Time and Money Freedom

This area is not just a list of the dollars in the bank or hours we want to sleep or weekend days we want to have off. It is tied back powerfully and authentically into who we are. What does more time mean to our lifestyle? For example, does stepping away from the office before 8 PM may mean having time to see our child's play, athletic event, recital? Maybe it gives you time to have a family dinner to connect without devices? Does it mean traveling to family members who live across the country or meeting up at a shared dream destination to deepen a connection at a beach, state park, or theme park?

For me, my vision is to downsize to a no maintenance place to travel without worry about the grass being unkept while I am gone. For some, they are looking for a backyard with a firepit to have family and neighbors over to roast marshmallows and catch fireflies. Others want the excitement of living in the city with a balcony overlooking the city lights and walking to their favorite restaurant or club to meet friends. There are as many permutations of this vision as there are people.

The idea is that just because we have a social business that does not mean that we do not have a need for a balanced life. Recharging ourselves and creating that unique definition of what balance means to each of us is the goal.

Evoke

Evoke Success Qualities

Beyond the mental faculty of imagination, which is woven throughout, the Slinky® evokes leadership qualities we strive to embody such as discernment, respect, resilience, flexibility, and abundance. We discern how the Slinky® moves at our direction and with inappropriate action can become bent or tangled. We learn respect for those boundaries and the science and engineering that went into this deceptively simple toy to sustain motion down a staircase and hang mid-air. We see the resilience designed for it to regain its original form. We can demonstrate flexibility through moving the Slinky® in various forms and positions. The enduring design of the product brought the owner's abundance.

Discernment is a Capability

Knowing where we are going or in more business terms defining our vision and business strategy, mission, product, service, process, and organization structure in terms everyone associated with the business can understand is essential. If we are in the launch stage, we may wear multiple hats officially, but we need to know where we will source the skills and capabilities, we are not skilled at.

Here is where "The Slinky® Effect" becomes more than a static picture in your mind, and it becomes a true moving, dynamic effect that we can adopt and adapt as a theme for how we make decisions in our business. When you hold the Slinky® in your hands, you control the expansion and contraction. For those of us who immediately leap to control, it is just is an illusion. We need to understand that we control four things: our intention, our attention, our actions, and our response. Leadership is not about controlling others; it is about these four elements and evoking the same behaviors through earned trust and respect by consistency.

Every day that we wake up, we choose what will occupy our attention. If we don't choose anything, habit will win by default, the Slinky® toy will sit on the shelf (or wherever we left it) contracted, unexpanded, and the results will be pretty much the same as the day before, week before, and the same as however long we choose to leave the Slinky® sitting on the shelf. We'll wake up and brush our teeth, have our coffee, take the same route to our office, follow our work calendar, our kids' events and carpool calendar, our to-do list, maybe watch a favorite TV show, lay in bed until we fall asleep then wake up rinse and repeat.

Respect is Earned

We know that respect is earned and granted and cannot be demanded. However, the actions we take, the attitude that we hold and how we show up every day is in our control. We decide if we operate with integrity and inclusion. We decide if we respect our customers, our business partners, and other relationships we hold with family and friends. Where we focus our attention produces the equal and opposite return. If we rush through the day focused on results, timelines, and profits, we will see those. If we focus on lifting as we climb, creating negotiations where both parties benefit then we receive that.

Evoke Resiliency

We all face failure; it is how we rebound that matters. We all know the quote by Thomas Edison "I have not failed. I've just found 10,000 ways that won't work." Think about what our lives would be like without all of the inventions he created. If we can visualize the idea, product, service, and business, it can be done. Just look at the seemingly absurd products that are out there. Here is just one of thousands of examples we can find on the internet. Having the belief in our idea, product, service, and business will serve as a foundation to get through the myriad of setbacks along the way.

Evoke Flexibility

Control has two sides: control our actions, decide the future, and attempt to control other influences, people, and the economy. One works and the other is an exercise in futility. Leadership is not about control. It is about belief, negotiation, and enrollment. We are all forms of energy and we sense the energy of others, even if we do not overtly recognize it. We call it charisma, kismet, and a variety of negative terms too. Our belief is an energetic state that can be generated. Once developed we can hold that state and transmit it as we negotiate and enroll support.

Evoke Abundance

We choose our vision and define what abundance means to us. The billionaires of the world define abundance differently than I do. This is a fact, or I would be a billionaire. I would have taken different actions and made different decisions to align my goals with that path. Earlier we highlighted our thought patterns. Once set, they act just as a thermostat on our home heating system. They allow a certain tolerance for variance, yet they kick in when we move outside of the pre-set range. If our thermostat is not set at the abundance level we desire, we will not achieve and sustain that level. Only a decision to reset the thermostat to a new greater level accompanied by the supporting actions to create new actions that are consistent with that desired level of abundance will work.

Explore

Encourage exploration

The Slinky® has been recognized over the years with many honors. It serves as a teaching tool in University Physics classes around the globe. The Slinky Dog® is once again featured in the 2019 release of Toy Story 4. Despite every young child having access to a smart device, radio-controlled trucks, computers, and dozens of other toys that keep them locked onto their device, the basic toys that inspire them to explore their imagination and creativity remain.

Recap of the Journey

Emerge - Mr. James did not just have a great idea; he took the sustained actions required to bring it into form. He worked over a year to develop the prototype. Then when that sold out in minutes, he knew he was on to something big. He took the actions to relocate to another state where he invented the manufacturing process.

We can emulate this same innovation launch process for our idea and leverage the access to not only our own ecosystem but the ecosystems of other subject matter experts in various forms of contracts, partnerships, and investors to incubate the idea into a market ready product or service for our business.

Extend – After its initial popularity at the Gimble's introduction, Mr. James had to go on to develop the mass-manufacturing machinery that could keep pace with the toy's popularity because the production equipment did not exist. Some would see this as an obstacle, but he viewed it as an opportunity.

Earlier in the book, we posed a plethora of questions. Every day, if we remain curious, we will come up with more. By continuing to answer those questions, we move from a paper business plan to a vibrant business model that acts as a framework to support our business today. That continuous focus on our value chain and our vision creates a framework that is extensible to weather the variances in market conditions, geopolitical forces, and the future of work.

Expand - The company went on to continue to expand. They added the Slinky Dog® as well as other colors and materials over time. This mindset of continuing to look for opportunities and growth is key to the long-term success for Slinky® and its other products.

Our idea today fits the needs of today's customers. A sustainable business is rarely built on only one product or service. Building the leadership capabilities, we have today, can serve as the basis for vetting new ideas, building the connections, networks, and processes that support our ability to expand and continue to answer the pull to growth.

Energize – The pre-compressed tension of the Slinky® prepares it for action and movement and the underlying math and science determine that this was no accident, it was the intentional desired outcome of the prototyping process to bring it into form.

Many of us love to learn, plan, and design. Those are vital needs, yet without converting that learning, planning, and designing into action, we are merely in motion, entertaining ourselves. The pull to growth requires intentional action in service of the vision, mission, milestones, and goals of the business. Without action, we contract and move into longing and discontent. When we notice these emotions showing up in our lives, it is time to set out on a course of action.

Empower – Another hallmark of the leadership and direction Mr. and Mrs. James provided over the years was to enter into an agreement with another inventor of the Rainbow Slinky®. The story of that product's development and manufacturing history within the company is quite interesting in itself. The idea for the Slinky Dog® was submitted by a customer and the company empowered the development of that idea.

Self-leadership is about giving ourselves permission to go for the big dream and bold move that will create global impact as a result of our company's success. Business leadership for your organization is about empowering the other relationships needed to drive and promote success. We model the behaviors and capabilities desired in our interactions, negotiations, and service.

Evolve – The underlying math and Hooke's Law and the effects of gravitation are the DNA if we will of the toy. It was evolved through nurture and care of the additional possibilities Mr. James saw when it fell off the worktable, he wanted it to be able to walk. Mr. James' imagination was sparked by the movement he saw when developing another spring for another purpose. Not everyone acknowledges the future of further development and refinement of the toy that was needed to fully evolve into the vision.

To evolve is different than to expand. To expand we keep the same foundation and offer more. To evolve, we identify what ideas, products, services, and even divisions of our business no longer fill a customer need and we replace them with something that better serves the need. Our discipline and discernment in reviewing the metrics of the business in conjunction with our analysis of the external factors and influencers is required to effectively evolve our leadership.

Evoke – The Slinky Dog® was selected by Pixar for inclusion in the original Toy Story movie. The company worked to reinvent the Slinky Dog® to update the look to match the feeling of the movie. They didn't compromise on the core principles of the toy and how the leash works but they made it a more friendly face to allow it to evoke the joy of the Slinky Dog® giving it new life in 1995 and continuing through the success of the movie franchise today.

We evoke our best selves to encourage the business to shepherd the ideas and create the business framework and relationships. We stumble and start over, but in doing so we not only achieve the desired outcome, but we become better leaders when we lift as we climb and earn the respect of our colleagues, staff, and business partners. We can evoke business alliances and partnerships that leverage our product or service to bring it to another set of customers and audiences.

Parting Thoughts

We decide what kind of legacy we want to build for our self as a leader and the business(es) we serve and create. Do we set our perspective, reason and other faculties on autopilot when we realize our initial vision, OR do we continue to honor our pull to growth through curiosity and exploration to see the possibilities that emerge and expand vision that energizes and empowers our team to evolve and evoke even greater outcomes that extend our legacy and footprint?

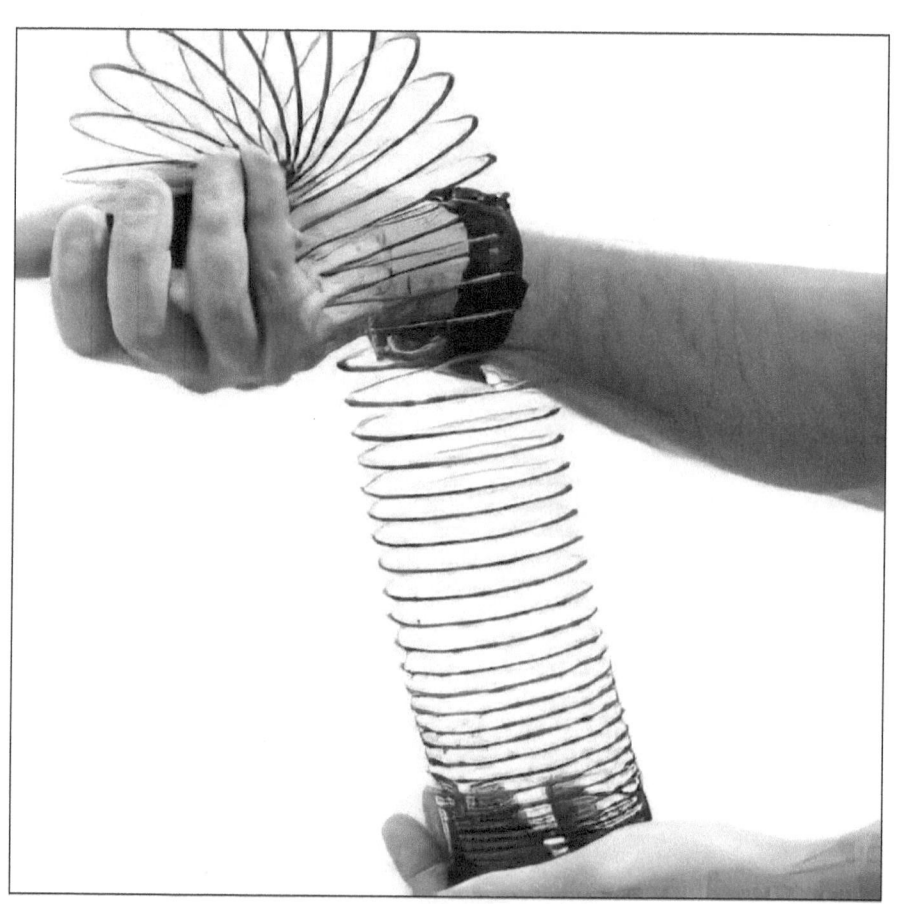

CHAPTER TWO
EMERGE

Design Your Startup or Recovery

We all a have an bit of an understanding that a design starts with a blueprint. It takes an idea and puts more detail behind it. For a home we move from a rough drawing on a piece of paper to formal architectural drawings. For a product we move from an idea to a patent or a trade secret to put the mechanics and math behind proving out the concept. Investors love to see ideas move from the rough idea stage to the blueprint stage as it formalizes the thinking and crystalizes the details.

Hypothetical Value to Real Value

I remember when a friend was telling me about the story of when his son came home one day in high school and told him he wanted to "day trade" along with some friends who were doing it. They opened a TD Ameritrade account and staked him with a small amount of money, enough to trade but not enough that if he lost it all it would be an issue. And off he went.

A few weeks later he asked "Dad, what is a PE ratio?" So, his Dad said to him "You know that deli that you stop in every morning to get a bacon, egg, and cheese on the way to school?" He said "Yes". I said "Let us say that tomorrow the owner says to you, I'm selling the business, do you want to buy it? My business makes $1 million a year in profits and has a record of doing that for the last thirty years". The dad asked his son, "How much would you pay him for it?" His son thought about it and said, "Four to five million dollars". His dad asked him why. He said, "Because I would get my money back in four to five years and then make a million dollars a year after that". I said, "You offered to pay a PE of 4 to 5". And he said, "Oh, I get it".

This story stayed with me because I never would have even considered learning finance at this boy's age. It is so impressive to see him lean in to trying something bold. I like to call that kind of valuation "real value". We pay $4-5 million for a business and we get our money back after a few years then cash flow after that. While nothing in life is guaranteed, real value is tangible. We can see our way to realizing it. It is right there in front of us.

Then there is what happens in early stage investing. We offer $1 million for 20-25% of a company and value it at the same $4-5 million. But there is no cash flow. There is no revenue. There are no customers. There is no product. Just a few people and an idea. That is hypothetical value. We think "If this becomes worth a billion dollars, we might hold onto half of our initial ownership and end up with $100 million or more". And we plunk down the money and go.

Here is the thing. A startup becomes a company and eventually, that company gets valued on real value metrics. Someday it will have customers, revenue, and profits. And investors will think "How many years of profits will I be willing to pay for that company?" A PE ratio will be applied, and it will be valued on the business fundamentals and not what can or could be.

Venture capitalists, seed funds, and angel investors make or lose money on the journey from hypothetical value to real value. And when the spread between the two narrows, we make less money. When the spread increases, we make more money.

It is easier to drink our own Kool-Aid in the world of hypothetical values. We handicap the odds of winning more aggressively. We trade ownership for capital at work. We accept the new normal.

Real value does not move so fast. Because it is right in front of us. We can see it. So, it is not prone to flights of fancy.

During the 2020 pandemic, the Small Business Association (SBA) was the vehicle used by legislation to fund a portion of the disruption caused by a temporary shutdown of the economy in the overarching interest of public health. Those businesses that had a sound business model and framework were able to be the first in line to present their application for these funds, because they had been following some or all of these principles in the short run. These funds were tied to specific targets and milestones that when properly accounted for and allocated, allowing these businesses to emerge from the disruption.

Let us try to keep this framework front and center in our brains as we meet with founders and work to find transactions that work for everyone. This can be a stabilizing force in an unstable startup market as you emerge your idea through the innovation launch process.

Emergence of the Idea from Inspiration

I saw on Facebook recently that a young boy of 10 years old was moved by the loss of a young child in his neighborhood. The child had been a victim of hot car death. He decided that he wanted to stop this from ever happening again. He has invented a small device that is mounted to the headrest over the seat where the child, regardless of the method, is strapped in. The device has two functions, when the child is left behind, it notifies the driver by a loud signal and it blows cool air on the child, while the driver is returning to the vehicle. His parents invested in developing a prototype and Toyota is interested in bringing the device to market. How cool is it that the child had the idea and that his parents did not discount the idea as unworkable because it came from a child's mind? They ran with it and supported turning the idea into something that is right and good for all.

This story example of how we can employ those same techniques when we recognize a new idea. We take an idea that rarely emerges fully intact and continue to refine the idea until it becomes an actionable concept. We also need to stay true to the idea in the face of adversity. An idea without action sits in readiness but never changes form like a Slinky® in its box or on the shelf. Our intention, attention, and action are what is required to take that idea forward. To bring it into fuller form. We essentially create everything twice, we flesh out the idea, then bring it into form.

Innovation is not just an Idea

When we take the next step and focus our intention, attention, and actions on monetizing an idea, it is the emergence of value creation, which is the desired outcome of this process. To develop a sound market-ready business, we begin with the end in mind. Here are a variety of techniques that can be employed as a framework for the ideation process: Challenging Assumptions, Dreaming, Redefining the Problem, Triggered Brain Mapping, Worst Idea, Intuiting Images.

I have learned that using a defined framework allows us to provide a clear set of directions to the group we are using to generate, refine, and select the idea. These boundaries let the participants know that all ideas are valued and how the process of prioritizing the ideas and refining them will occur so that all participants feel valued and align their behaviors during the process to support the outcome. Ideation is a process and while we can do this as an individual exercise, we can also use these techniques with our fellow leaders or teams.

Challenging Assumptions

Each of us has developed our unique perspective based on our environment, influences, successes, and failures. These thought patterns become assumptions about how the customer will accept the idea, the readiness of the market to support an idea, and our acceptance of what ideas will work. The point of this framework is to set the expectations that these assumptions will be challenged. What if statements, invitations, and other techniques for facilitators are needed to keep the exercise about the assumption and not about the person putting forth the assumption?

Here is an example of challenging an assumption. A major auto manufacturer was looking for new lines of business. All of their divisions within their business model dealt with new model design, build, and the distribution processes. They designed and built their own parts, bought some new parts from selected OEM vendors, and assembled the resulting vehicle for distribution to their network of dealerships. In collaborating with them to challenge these assumptions and models, we worked with an idea to develop a green venture, which was pioneering in 1999. The resulting idea was to establish a network of junk yards to identify newer models that had been damaged in accidents and harvest the remaining valuable parts to be refurbished, inventoried, and recycled for resale to their customer base and dealerships online. After a few weeks we had the strategy, business plan, and the client were ready to issue competitive bids for technology vendors to implement the supporting technology.

To employ this technique yourself, we will need to assemble 20 or more assumptions worded in such a way that the group can provide a true or false opinion. For a new product or service, select the assumptions that relate to market entry. To develop this framework in other contexts and to expand or evolve, look at all aspects of the business. The selected assumptions are the discussion starters to generate new ideas that challenge the assumption.

Dreaming

The goal is to generate wildly ambitious ideas, the bigger, more audacious, the better. When facilitating this, set the expectation that nothing is off-limits or too crazy for round one. When the group has compiled 20 or more ideas, move to the next step. Playing small rarely leads to exponential growth and innovation. It can lead to continuous improvement and other goal attainment actions. Our mission as leaders of innovation is to be bold and brave. We want to encourage our participants with the idea: What if you could not fail? This brings out their creativity, rather than their concern for how the peers and colleagues will view them.

I led the development of a proposed solution for a global nonprofit client that was looking for a solution that enabled their project managers working in remote locations across five continents to be able to share data in near time. I assembled a team from across the organization to ideate all aspects of the solution. We put ourselves in the shoes of a project manager and identified the need for portability (more of an issue in 2005 than today), security to make sure the technology and user did not become theft targets, and connectivity. Beyond that we looked at the type of projects they managed, contagious disease treatment, food insecurity, housing, disaster recovery, war, and famine, and we could see these were big important issues. We designed an approach that the nonprofit could use to solicit feedback from their project managers around the globe leveraging their social networks, web conferences, and other tools to elicit their requirements before we launched the design process of the solution.

Facilitate the discussion to select the most viable ideas from the list, regardless of who provided the idea. The facilitator asks the participants to adopt a variety of different perspectives during the exercise. Let them respond as themselves and their role in the company relationship at first. Then as conversation ebbs, ask them to adopt the perspective of someone from another planet, another country, or whatever will stimulate the sourcing of new ideas from this fresh perspective. Adopting a role other than ourselves is more freeing for quieter participants. The end result of this exercise is a prioritized list of ideas to pursue.

Redefine the Problem

The same thinking that created the problem cannot be used to solve it. This technique helps participants move out of the thought patterns that created the problem by facilitating the process for reframing it in a new context, allowing for the opportunity to gain experience and provide value. We know that as human beings, we all face two types of constraints on a daily basis. The first is circumstantial, which are all external constraints (budget, resources, support, and time). It is easy to focus on only this constraint. However, we all have inner constraints. We will delve into how we developed our patterns of behavior in upcoming parts of the book. Success in leadership is understanding when the old patterns have served their purpose and new operating patterns can be adopted. This increases our focus on how we can change our perspective and look at constraints as an opportunity in disguise.

We had successfully launched a state-based marketplace for a newly formed agency. During the software development we had created a number of use cases and the solution met all those needs. However, we failed to imagine the exceptions that might arise. One exception was that enrollment began on October 1 for coverage that started on January 1 and life happens. People who are enrolled die and no longer need coverage, but their surviving spouse still does. People get divorced. The business rules of the system did not permit making these changes in a straightforward manner. We came up with two problem statements. The first was how do we minimize the impact for the clients who experience these situations. The second was how do we redesign the system to accommodate these life events. We set up a laptop and projector to go into the development environment of the software and see if there was a sequence of steps we could take in the software as designed that would drop the enrollment of the deceased or divorced spouse while continuing the enrollment of the remaining spouse. After a bit of trial and error, we found the sequence. Then we replicated it and documented each step to determine that it was not a fluke and to use in training a staff of 5,000 workers. We also noted that this frequently impacted the rates for the surviving spouse as the income of the other spouse had to be excluded for future years. The next step was to show the workaround to the developers. They could visualize the possibilities for changing the software code and adding user fields to facilitate how this could be accomplished more elegantly. As a percentage of all enrollments this was small, but the several hundred or so people impacted were appreciative and did not have to deal with the frustration consumers in other states did when their solution could not accommodate these changes and incorrect coverage and bills were generated every month.

Tips for how to facilitate this approach: develop a clear statement of the problem. An example might be "Five people die every hour from opioid overdoses". This is a daunting problem that haunts us in every state. Next, we reframe that problem into an opportunity. We can stop legal opioid prescription abuse by developing a nationwide database of all prescriptions and analyze the patterns. Next the group starts developing highly calibrated What questions to break down the statement into action-focused ideas. What parameters need to be identified to identify legal opioid use from abuse? What patterns emerge around abuse (excess free time, professions that cause injuries, lack of knowledge)? The answers to these questions become the requirements for the database. It also may promote additional opportunities. The foster care system is overburdened due to the impacts of opioid abuse. These additional opportunities should be captured, and another session scheduled to source opportunities for our business to keep the flow of the original topic moving forward.

Triggered Brain Mapping

The technique starts with multiple expressions of the problem the group is attempting to solve through ideation. The goal is to leverage the power of language to stimulate creativity. A CPA notices a challenge in a high seasonal revenue variance. They begin to frame it initially as I need more revenue. Framing the questions in different ways can open perspectives for creating an opportunity: What new services can I offer? How can I enroll my tax clients in other services I offer? What are passive revenue streams I can create to get steady year-round revenue? The quality of our business leadership is often measured by the quality of the questions we ask.

A water authority I worked with posed the initial challenge, "How can we promote conservation of water usage without adversely impacting our revenue?" We turned this into different challenges to look at all aspects of their business model. How can we detect leakage in the infrastructure early to minimize water loss? How can we vary our billing structure to reward conservation? Can we identify additional products and services that generate revenue not tied to water consumption? How can we review our licensing and permitting requirements to reward green development projects? This engaged the senior level executives from all divisions to come up with ideas both in their area of expertise and crazy ideas that other areas might consider.

To facilitate we can do this via written notes on flipcharts or verbally in a circle with a pad of paper circulating. In the first technique the group posts their thoughts on the wall for each expression. Then after the first round, everyone takes time to circulate and review the first round of comments and add new thoughts that were stimulated by other people's responses. It continues until there are no new ideas. The pad of paper process is conducted by circulating the pad in rounds until all ideas are captured.

Worst Idea

This technique is a great for an icebreaker for people who do not normally work together to get people laughing and to release tension of the expected outcome. It also works well for groups that have been working together for a long period of time to shake up expectations. The goal is to generate a list of bad ideas and then keep going for worse and worst. By starting with this exercise, we reinforce the point that there are no bad ideas and all ideas are welcome.

At another state, we are a day behind in meeting our stress and volume test metrics for our client. The client sponsor had a meeting with the Governor the next day. She went with what we thought would be the worst idea, not to use the worker portal for client interactions. My role then became, how do we make this work? Training is underway, materials are developed, and we are two weeks away from going live. For the next eight hours, we identified every task that could not be performed in the consumer portal and how the workflow should be rerouted to send those client calls and meetings to workers who would use the original portal. We limited the software changes and relied on training, job aids, and in-field support to have the workers use the other portal. By adopting the worst idea and fully committing to its success, we mobilized all of the resources needed for a successful launch.

To facilitate we really push the group to keep throwing out bad ideas because this can be uncomfortable for executives who innately cast out seemingly bad ideas without serious consideration. Once we have a good list then we ask the group to find a seed of good in each idea. This shakes up thinking and stimulates imagination. It is counterintuitive and serves to both break the existing thought patterns each participant brings to the table, and in the end, we will be surprised at the potential for a good idea to emerge from this exercise.

Intuiting Images

This technique works well in solving marketing and communication problems. Depending on our leadership type and the participants it can easily be used for other problems too. An example may be when our product or service is an evolutionary leap forward from what is on the market today and there are limited comparisons, so we need to build understanding as well as awareness.

This exercise can be very useful in working with marketing, web designers, and other people to evoke the brand story that not only resonates with us as a business leader but in gathering feedback from a user experience perspective to see what ideas are generated about how our brand is perceived, specifically whether we have identified their true problem and the corresponding best idea to solve it.

Tips for facilitating define the problem and pre-select 10 or more images from a free online image source. Make sure at least one image is random and does not necessarily correspond to the idea at a surface level. If we are applying in a technology context, select images that correspond similarly with retail, manufacturing, and healthcare. Images are great at stimulating imagination and intuition, so be prepared for great ideas.

Honing the Idea

Now is the time to put the idea through its paces. Do the customer research to understand market size, income, and other demographics for how to reach your target market/demographic. Research our competition. If there is no competition, it is likely there is a limited market, if any. If that is the case, do we have the wherewithal to create a market, like Apple did with the PC?

Crystalizing the idea into an actionable concept is next. In essence we are creating an elevator pitch for our product or service. We want to quickly communicate exactly what the idea is in 30 seconds or less. An example is: My product is _____. It does _____ better/faster/cheaper than anything else. Keep refining until we get to that level of clarity and precision.

The final step in ideation is to gain external validation. Presuming that we conducted the exercises above with an internal audience from our company, now is the time to validate with other business relationships before moving to the next step. The safe part is done and now the rubber meets the road by seeking opinions of potential customers.

Incubation Makes Your Idea a Marketable Product and Service

The genesis of the incubation has been around for decades. In a formal program a public sector entity, university, or for-profit venture takes applications for participation in their program. The program usually has a defined set of startup businesses they want to work with. These fall into the categories of high-tech, low-tech, and non-tech ideas. A new app, new software, and/or device are high-tech examples. Low technology examples are manufactured goods because the technology is required for product production but is not the actual product. A 3D printed chair, medical device, or other products are good examples. Non-tech ideas are businesses such as real estate and services businesses.

While these are amazing programs and are a good fit for startup businesses, the focus for this section is on extrapolating those processes used in that structured setting as a framework for incubating our idea and bringing it into form. This process is similar to bringing home a new child. We do not just put them in their new bed, shut the door, and wait for them to grow up. That is absurd on the face of it, yet somehow, we think that random attention to the new idea will bring amazing results. As technology developers, engineers, and designers, what you create will impact the world we live in. To help solve the global issues we face today, it is more important than ever to invent products and services that help people and the world.

Inventing green can mean inventing a technology whose whole purpose is sustainability (like carbon sequestration or eliminating waste) or it can mean improving the environmental impacts of ordinary products, from material choice to energy use to changing users' lifestyles. For many companies, being environmentally responsible is also good business. By using a mindset of "inventing green," you can: save material costs with more efficient production methods; reduce liability risks associated with the manufacture or disposal of toxic materials; and meet customer demand for products that are safer for their families or less energy-intensive to use.

Whole system mapping is one process we can review to apply the four steps and the fundamental principles as we transform our idea into our prototype product. This process is recommended by NESsT.org (https://www.nesst.org).

Sketch a mind-map of your product's (or service's) whole system - the map needs to include the following features: the product's major components and how they connect (a full bill of materials or at least major subassemblies; if a service or digital product, what hardware is used?), the product's full life cycle (raw material, manufacturing, transport, use, disposal), and when / why / how the user uses the product or service. Adding arrows between the component Post-It notes demonstrates how the system's components are connected. This shows the flow of time, material, or logic. If other products or infrastructure are always used with your product or service (like clothes for a dryer or roads for a car), include them in the map, too.

Post-it notes on a whiteboard or big sheet of paper are best so that you can move things around as you build the map. For illustration purposes we will look at a commonly used product, a refrigerator, rather than a new high-tech product to visualize the output on the wall. A good eraser and whiteboard work too.

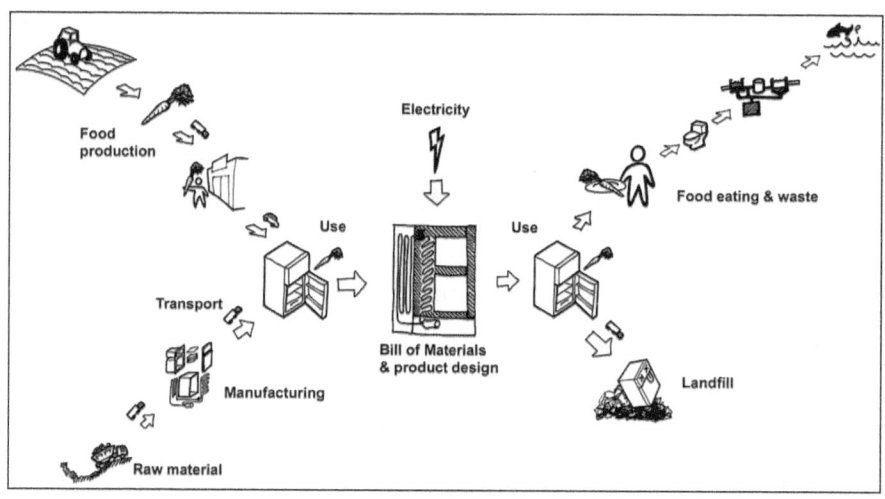

Image Credit: Faludi MCAD Class (2010)

Set priorities based on Life Cycle Assessment (LCA) and our business model - There are a variety of LCA tools on the internet. Take some time to review and see what model most closely resembles your industry, product, and components in the map. This research will save time in modifying the tool to your business down the road. To set priorities, quantitatively measure the biggest opportunities to improve your product. This exercise uses a basic estimated life cycle assessment (LCA). However, learning LCA takes time, so here are some alternatives:

- Use a mini-LCA quiz to get some ideas about types of metrics you might track
- Explore certification systems (like Cradle to Cradle or EPEAT)
- Find an existing LCA someone else conducted and published online
- Use one of the graphs below to fake it for this exercise

Since the point of this is not to teach you LCA, we will save time and concentrate on this design method. We choose the product category closest to ours in the graphs below and use it to find your top sustainability priority. Each graph below is a rule-of-thumb for general categories of products; for precision decisions, use an LCA for your actual product.

For example, the refrigerator above would be in the "large electrical" category, so its top priority would be energy use during its life. For this and your own estimated LCAs, remember they will always have large uncertainties, so you should only trust large differences in scores.

Sample LCA Model

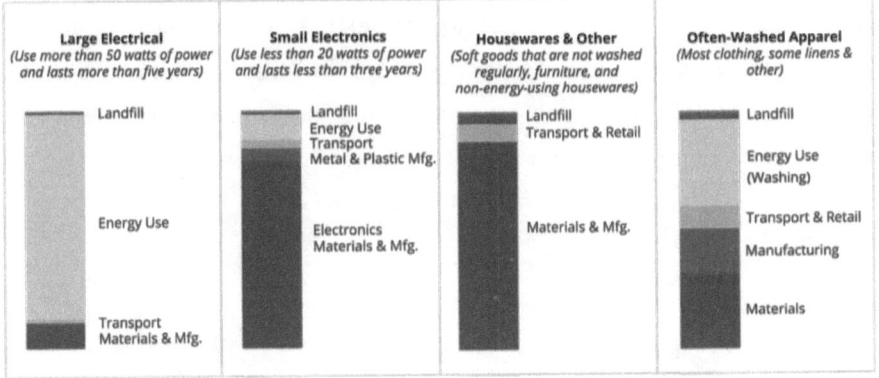

Image Credit: Faludi MCAD Class (2014)

Given your estimated LCA, first write down your top environmental problem to focus on. You may also write down a top social sustainability problem to focus on if you know one. Second, write down one or two non-sustainability business priorities (e.g. price, necessary features, etc.). Clearly number the priorities in order of importance. You may list more sustainability and business priorities, but only two to four priorities keep it simple. The goal is not to leverage our advanced algorithm development skills, it is to identify where in our supply chain we can make a social impact by selecting the right vendor, features, or design to achieve our stated vision for how the product will serve the customer.

Brainstorm solutions on your system map - Now this is the fun part! Brainstorm on your Whole System Map from Step 1 to solve your top priority. For example, if your LCA shows that your product's energy use causes the most environmental damage and your business prioritizes low cost and visual appeal, your brainstorm's goal might be - reduce lifetime energy impacts without compromising cost or aesthetics.

Ideally, brainstorm using a different color of post-it than you did to make the system map, so you can tell your new ideas from the system components. Follow the rules of brainstorming to generate ideas: do not say no to any ideas, but also stay focused on your topic. Use the whole system map to:

Brainstorm at least one new idea for every key component (subassembly, component, or step in the process, Post-It note) in the system map. You should have several ideas for each relevant node, and ideally one for every node, relevant or not! This will help you have you a more thorough brainstorm. For example, here is a start for the refrigerator example we are using:

Whole System Map Example

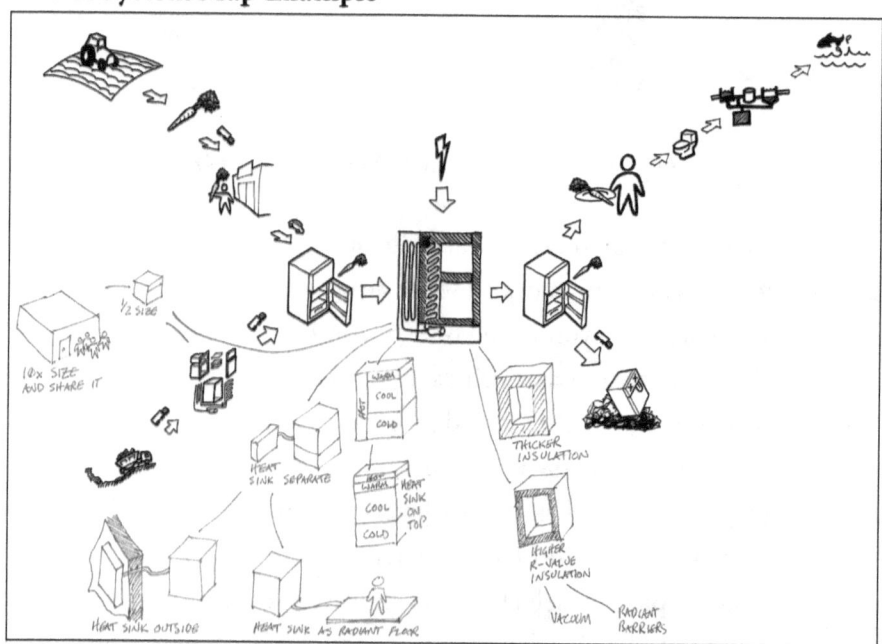

Image Credit: Faludi MCAD Class (2010)

All the ideas above relate to saving energy because when it comes to the refrigerator, energy use is the biggest environmental impact. However, this brainstorm still needs ideas for raw materials, electricity, and other nodes in the system map.

Brainstorm ways to eliminate current components in the system map to simplify and reduce risk and price as we noted in our earlier non-sustainable business priorities. This process of elimination gives you more radical ideas: the more nodes you skip, the more radical the idea usually becomes. For example, the brainstorm below has several ideas eliminating the refrigerator entirely and one idea eliminating the food supply chain. Generate at least five (ideally ten) ideas that skip components in the system.

Brainstorm Version of System Map

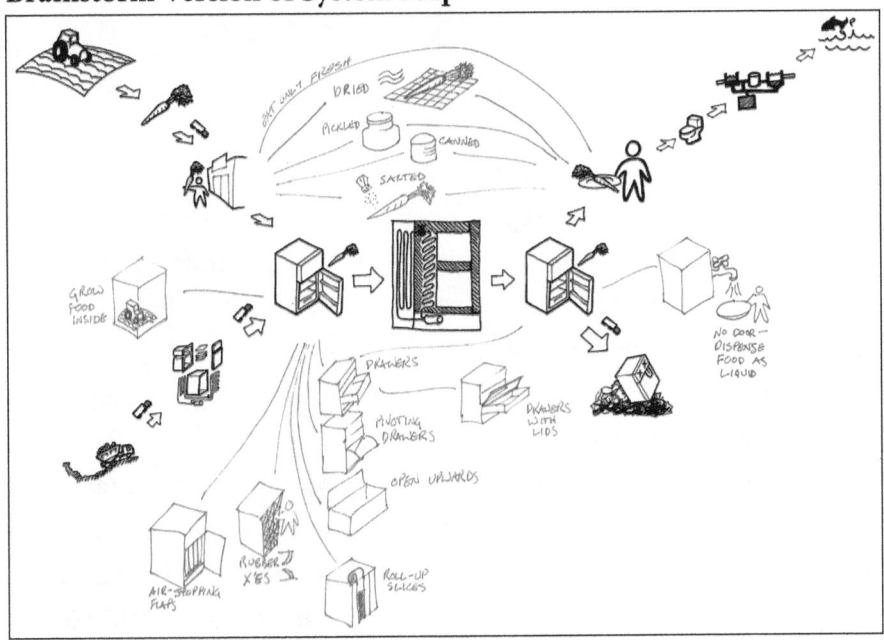

Image Credit: Faludi MCAD Class (2010)

If you want to get more advanced, you can integrate other systems-thinking methods into your brainstorm as we discussed in the ideation section earlier. This can be used to enhance your system map.

Choose a winning idea based on your priorities - take your brainstormed list of ideas and narrow it down to five to eight of the best options, considering what would best accomplish the priorities and delight users.

Then measure each of your top options against your Step 2 top priorities for sustainability and business. If you have LCA skills, do an estimated LCA on each. (Remember these results will have huge uncertainties so only trust huge improvements!) In choosing your final winner, balance sustainability and business priorities. One good way is to decide is to make a matrix like this:

Objective	Weight	Idea #1	Idea #2	Idea #3	Idea #4	Idea #5	etc...
Design Brief priority #1	5	3	2	5	1	1	...
Design Brief priority #2	5	1	5	4	4	2	...
Design Brief priority #3	3	3	3	3	5	5	...
Design Brief priority #4	2	5	5	3	3	3	...
etc...	...	...	...	...	...	...	...
Total Score		39	54	60	46	36	

Image NESsT.org

In this decision matrix, each column is one of your new ideas and each row is one of your design priorities. You might even add a row for "unique differentiator" to capture inspiring factors your design priorities miss. Score each option from 1 (bad) to 5 (best). Then multiply that score by the weight of how important that objective is, from 1 (do not really care) to 5 (top priority) and add up all the weighted scores. In the example table above, Option #3 wins.

This process involves intuition—that is why the decision matrix is valuable. It helps you juggle many estimates at the same time. You can use a different way of deciding on the winning idea instead of a decision matrix. You can also combine ideas or decide to pursue multiple ideas. The goal is to validate your intuition with reason based on analysis/estimation of each top option's performance versus your design priorities.

Now that you've finished the whole design method, you should have a clearer idea of the problem(s) you're solving and their context, a clearer set of priorities, lots of new ideas, and a decision of what to pursue further.

Now that we have a clear understanding of the whole system map, we can develop a prototype production plan. We identify the major milestones in securing the development of each of the components in the whole system map and schedule them in sequential order. If your whole system map is as complex as the example presented, MS Project or a similar tool while help you sequence tasks across the various areas of the business and work.

The most successful entrepreneurs insert those tasks their calendar. Often when we see the activities in list form, even with hours attached, we get overly ambitious and do not create time in the calendar for a full spectrum life. We need to adjust the project plan to fit the available hours in our calendars after we consider the other activities involved in the startup effort, our existing commitments to income, relationships, health, and time off. This is how we justify each position of every activity on our calendar. If we want to have a business and life that we value and love, we must be comfortable with our calendar as a means of support and structure rather than a weight that drags us down.

There is always a generative tension in a well-constructed calendar. It focuses us on the value-added tasks and also serves as a reminder as we review each day to see how much we accomplished. The real costs are even bigger though, such as lost market opportunity to competitor advantage, lost earnings potential while we pursue the idea part-time.

These steps in the innovation launch are also about developing the business leadership mindset of embedding these capabilities into our business models as our businesses move beyond the emerge state and into the various forms of growth over time. If you are using MS Project, create a section for each of these tasks in the overall plan and at the end of the book, you will have a complete plan for building your business with action steps identified.

Note that this is a great process to undertake, even if your new idea or product is not a green initiative, you can just do a quick cursory pass of the LCA step. It may yield more benefits than you initially anticipated and may broaden the appeal of your idea or product and increase its marketing potential.

Avatar Customer Identification

When we begin with the end in mind, one of the key outcomes is a satisfied customer. In the previous exercise we focused on what their problem or need was, now we move into further defining who they are. Creating an avatar customer is not just the new trendy name for target customer. It is about constructing an avatar that can be visualized. That visualization informs aspects of the book because it informs the prototyping of our product or service to fit them to a tee.

Demographics – we identify the gender, race, age, income, disabilities, mobility (in terms of travel time to work or number of vehicles available), educational attainment, home ownership, employment status, and even location. When we understand these specifics, we know the features that are needed. If a product improves access for a customer who has some form of physical limitation, then we can build in feature that enable their effective usage of the product. Home ownership may be important if our product is paint or building supplies. Targeting a neighborhood of apartment owners will not yield the desired outcome as they rarely invest in improving their rental property, so we want to target the owners of the property.

Income is a key point of knowledge. If we are building a new app for a smart device, it is important to know the pricing before we determine the app's features. High income people may be looking more for applications that improve convenience and efficiency, so they would see view games as a waste of time. Middle income customers may be looking for apps that aggregate savings to increase their buying power or improve their experience. Lower income customers will also be looking at savings but at a different level, they also may be interested in apps that increase their earning potential.

For a business dealing in real estate it is easy to see that a low maintenance, single story unit may be more appealing to a customer in a wheelchair than a multi-story dwelling with stairs and narrow doorways. Taking the time to create the avatar now can head off fatal design flaws later.

Now that we know who they are, we can understand how to reach them. If we are marketing business to business, identify the trade or industry organizations they participate in so we can show up there too. We now know language resonates with them, such as communicating our understanding of their needs and our ability to fulfill them. If we are global, we may need translation and specialized marketing services to reach various groups through effective cultural resonance. We cannot satisfy their need if we cannot reach them.

Beyond the crafting of a resonant, authentic message, an understanding of the media outlets they use is critical to deliver the message. Identifying which internet, radio, social media, trade publications, written media, or podcast is a cost-effective way to reach our target versus broad spectrum media blasts on channels that are not targeted to our audience. It is important to understand that the owner of the platform owns their data and does not always to share with us the differences in audience a by time of day program.

The final piece is in understanding them well enough to set up the correct nurturing strategy. We are all inundated by unwanted emails and robocalls that are the result of an undifferentiated marketing approach. If we want to build a long-term relationship with the customer, we need to understand their buying habits and preferences by looking at engagement versus list size as an appropriate metric for success. They purchased our product or service or at least exhibited curiosity; the goal is to understand the frequency and message that builds on that rather than repelling them.

Business Validation

During this segment of incubation, we focus on the product or service and making it the best it can be. Rapid prototyping is the most efficient for this approach. It also varies in duration and complexity based on our business. We will address how to build this capability at a high level by business type.

High-tech – this prototyping consists of identifying the requirements for the application and software and sharing them with the prototype developer. It will vary by complexity of the technology required. For an application, the basic requirements may be the function of the app, design look and feel, and any other avatar customer specific feature we identified in the previous step.

For a full software product there may be user design documents, specification of the underlying technology such as blockchain, artificial intelligence, python, etc. that are best suited to protect security, define business rules and regulations, add a payment option, and encourage ongoing learning. There are also ethical considerations. An application that uses patient record data to accelerate the elimination of a disease is a worthy goal. However, a decision is needed about whether that data is just accessed not stored. If stored, how is the data anonymized for storage and secured. Usability is another key design outcome to be incorporated into the overall product prototype.

Low-tech – the prototyping of a product can be an expensive investment. The advancement of 3D printing makes this technology affordable. Small businesses can now work with existing manufacturing vendors to create a prototype. This is a good example of how to quickly produce a small quantity of a product to use in focus groups for feedback. The value gained can be immeasurable as going straight to production may not only be cost-prohibitive, but also may not be feasible. The key to success is in building the ecosystem of partners, resources, and production capable vendors that enable this process.

Product design specifications are developed based on initial research into the best method for solving the business need. Then the specifications are socialized with prospective builders of the prototype. After contract negotiation and detailed review of the specifications, the builder creates the prototype. A focus group then uses the prototype and provides constructive feedback about what works and does not. The rapid prototype process looks to accelerate the frequency of the prototype iterations. The result is a verified product.

Forecasting demand is the next step. This will help us finalize the contract with the vendor who will build our product. Price, seasonality, and access to and execution of top marketing strategies will provide additional insight.

No-Tech – refers to the product or industry. Real estate, carpentry, electrician, CPA, health, and wellness centers are examples of these types of businesses. Here the prototyping may consist more of building a portfolio of past work, building a model of the type of building for an architect, or conducting a beta course for a teacher or coach. Here again the feedback on the prototype is solicited and iterations of the prototype are executed until the final product receives reviews. A long-term production strategy is needed here too. For those who are service-oriented, this may be implementing a strong calendar system and/or project management system that matches our capacity for taking on new projects. For example, a carpenter may take on a project to renovate a staircase or kitchen cabinets. They need to take the estimated time to produce the product for the customer and log the actions and any other factors into their project plan and calendar to understand, when the phone rings, what availability they have for their other customers. To work one customer at a time limits growth an expansion capability as our current customers refer people and we market our skills to attract new customers.

When speaking with a real estate investment broker the other day, he said that he thought because he bought and sold apartment buildings, this step could be skipped. However, he has a unique point of view on how he buys and develops his target properties. He targets larger, older unit properties in established neighborhoods. He limits the investment dollars for rehabilitation to modernization, not gentrification of the units, so that his current renters can still afford the units and will not be displaced, then he adds beneficial services that attract a higher caliber of tenant going forward. These may be adding an after-school program, community garden, or other low investment services that create a community and entice his renters to stay longer. This leads to higher occupancy and renter retention, reducing the need for heavy marketing. This is a great example of a no-technology prototype.

Regardless of the business type, the more clarity and belief in the quality of the product we are producing is essential for the investment process.

Business Plan – the development of the business plan is critical in a variety of ways that promote success. It focuses attention on the legal structures that best serve our business. For IRS purposes we have all of the responsibilities for any of the following structures to hold board meetings, draft minutes, document major business activities, and complete all filings. The goal is business separation. I am not the corporation and the corporation are not me.

Entrepreneurs can get caught up in the idea and building of the prototype to the exclusion of building a strong foundation. Yet, minimizing risk by paying attention to these important but not necessarily exciting details can be costly. The IRS can file a lawsuit that would strip away our privacy and protections if we are not careful. Here are the fundamentals for selecting the correct corporate structure for our venture. Even for existing companies, these concepts are important as we may choose to launch the new product under a new structure.

Sole Proprietorship – this allows the business owner to report their income from their business on a single tax return, all bets are off for tax benefits, privacy, and lawsuit protection.

Limited Liability Company - A limited liability company is the US-specific form of a private limited company. It is a business structure that can combine the pass-through taxation of a partnership or sole proprietorship with the limited liability of a corporation. These are currently extremely popular as they provide the separation and tax benefits desired by small businesses.

S Corporation – This must be filed within 90 days of the inception of our business. It is ideal for closely held companies because the advantage is that we can be an employee of the corporation for tax purposes.

C Corporations – are best for companies that want to move money between entities, allow stock ownership for investors, set your fiscal year, and have increased privacy and control. We will see this structure frequently in well-known companies such as Coca-Cola.

B Corporations - certified B Corporations are businesses that meet the highest standards of verified social and environmental performance, public transparency, and legal accountability to balance profit and purpose. B Corps are accelerating a global culture shift to redefine success in business and build a more inclusive and sustainable economy.

After the business legal formation and structure are selected, the proper format of the business plan document can be selected to track the financial forecasting and projections we will develop. Here is where key decisions such as pricing and volume projections to track anticipated revenue and demands are captured. It also documents the costs of the business. Direct Cost of Goods Sold (COGS) are costs that correspond directly to the production and distribution of our product and service. The cost of the prototype development and future production costs are documented here. Indirect COGS are costs such marketing, rent, purchase payment for our brick and mortar facilities, technology (not related to a product), salaries, commissions, benefits, or contractor fees.

We will document our processes and approach for all major functions of the business including our mission, vision, and our strategy for accomplishing our forecasted success. The statistics of four of five small business startups failing in the first year are daunting. Yet, small businesses account for 83% of all new job creation and 50% of the US GDP.is generated by companies of under 50 employees.

"Everyone can tell we the risk. An entrepreneur can see the reward!" – Robert Kyosaki

Business Fundamentals are the difference between success and failure of the business. Risks everywhere are an initiative-taking, structured approach that are essential as a business leader. We will see risk in the form of

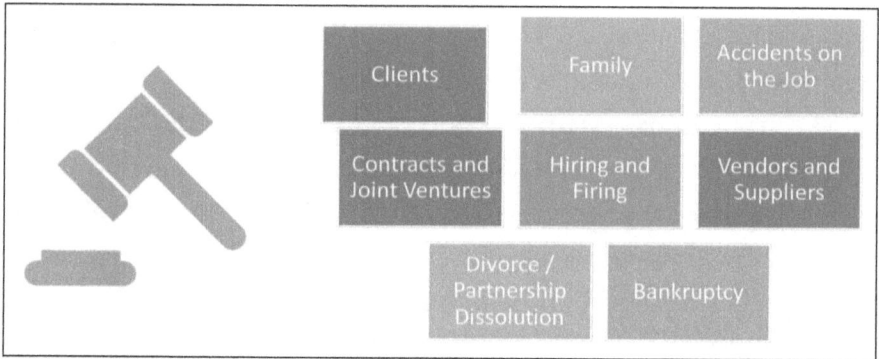

These and other scenarios result in a lawsuit being filed every 22 seconds. We can continue to put ourselves at risk as business owners or we can focus our attention on the initiative-taking. Our first step is deciding the correct business structure to remove risk and enable growth.

"Risk comes from not knowing what you are doing". – Warren Buffet

Protecting our corporate veil is as critical as advancing the cool big idea. If we are not a business owner that loves to hold and document meetings or resolutions decisions, there are companies who focus on do it for we service. Do not delude yourself that because you are new, small, or whatever form of denial you are in. Fifty-seven percent of all lawsuits are against businesses making $1M or less. Why? Because we are often seduced into setting aside the critical business functions and structures for the fun parts of being in business.

As a result of the work we have done up until now we have accumulated a variety of assets that need to be protected. By thinking strategically and identifying our risks up front, we can protect these assets and reduce the incentive to be sued. Investing now is far more cost effective than paying later.

IP Assets – These can increase the value of our company. Oftentimes up to as 80% of the value of our company is in Intellectual Property and is used in both investment funding and exit strategies. There are business entity strategies based on John D. Rockefeller's philosophy "Own Nothing, But Control Everything" that we can create to insulate our IP and other business assets . These structures are great for privacy lawsuit protection. They protect our assets, leave a legacy, and reduce risk of losing what we own.

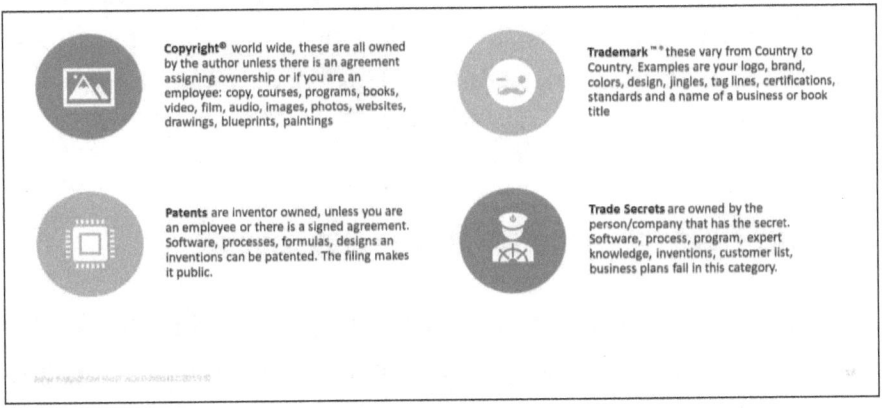

Company Culture – is defined by the business leader. We will discuss this in more detail in future chapters. At this point the focus is on creating our KPIs and other metrics and tools such as a Balanced Scorecard, in alignment with the culture we are creating. Amazon only has four metrics and they are all related to customer experience and fulfillment. They align and support each other, which has provided the ability to expand, extend, and evolve.

Business Relationships - We will see that in the risk category we reviewed earlier, business relationships are a driver of lawsuits, both frivolous and with merit. The same focus and attention on proactively gaining expert review, assuming we do not have our law degrees, can head off disputes that cost us in several ways. There are the customer reviews, delayed production and delivery and opportunity cost of growing our business instead of putting out fires and lawsuits.

Sales – document how we will sell and scale to meet the figures in our plan. Decide if we are all online, if are we offline in brick and mortar facilities, or a combination of the above. As our marketing investment and effort gains traction, customers need to know how and where to find us. Define what supporting customer service we will have to support the 24-hour per day availability of attracting our target customer online. We will talk more about our health, wellness, and relationship impacts if we do not have these processes put in place before we launch our product.

The key takeaway from the business plan step in the process is if we do not love doing these tasks, find and develop the appropriate business relationship with someone who does. This is not optional and a key source of risk and value for our business.

Emerge Financial Viability through Investment

Now that we have taken our idea and built a great product and a solid business plan, it is time to ground our idea and product from the hypothetical and look at our financial options. Here are some thoughts around how to understand, articulate, and manage the potential valuation gap between our hypothetical valuation and real market valuation.

Recently I was talking to an entrepreneur that is raising an investment round and the topic of valuation came up. Valuation is always a sensitive issue. Entrepreneurs, rightly so, figure they should get the highest valuation possible. Investors, on the other side, want the lowest valuation possible that still wins the deal. Only, we are in unusual times with valuations at or near their all-time highs (excluding the dot com days, of course).

Entrepreneurs need to mind the valuation gap. The valuation gap is the delta between what the public market multiples currently support (run rate) and the valuation (run rate) private investors are willing to invest. For example, if super high growth SaaS companies trade at 8x run-rate on the public markets, and an entrepreneur raises money from an investor at 12x run-rate, there is a 50% valuation gap.

Assuming superb execution, the startup will grow into the valuation and skip over the gap. For entrepreneurs, the risk is raising at too high a valuation and not growing into it. One of the worst possible outcomes for a venture-backed startup on the fundraising treadmill is to have a down round. Startups are essentially broken when they raise a new round of funding at a valuation lower than their last round. The strategy for entrepreneurs finds a balance between the best valuation possible and the best valuation that ensures a strong likelihood of a higher valuation in the next round. There is no right or wrong answer, but there is often an answer that makes it easier to sleep well at night — find that one.

One of our knowledge points is to understand the dilution dance for each financing round. Ten years ago, when we went out to market to raise money for our startup business or a new venture within an existing business potential investor, we talked about wanting to buy 33-40% of the business in the Series A. As an entrepreneur, the thought of selling that big of a chunk in one single round bothered us as entrepreneurs, and we mostly ended up passing. Fortunately, we were able to get to a nice exit without raising institutional capital. Now, typical funding rounds are in the 15-30% dilution range, not counting growing the employee option pool, which usually adds 5% more dilution.

Today, entrepreneurs have more choices. Options like revenue financing and finding investors that will do straight secondary financing, providing more liquidity for the entrepreneur. This creates more varied pools of money that we as creative entrepreneurs can build and leverage, such as family offices doing venture-like deals which was unheard of in the past. It is a great time to be an entrepreneur.

Another feature of today's market is that we can sell even smaller chunks of the business, especially if the startup is considered "hot". Investors are sitting on so much cash, many of the rules like "I need to own

20% of the company" no longer apply. If you want to sell 10% of the startup, many more investors are likely interested, assuming it meets their criteria.

Entrepreneurs would do well to find the balance between selling as little of their startup as possible and raising enough money to reach their next milestone or inflection in the business. Times are good, so it is advisable to raise a little extra, but of course that's extra dilution as well. There is a dilution dance with each financing round, and entrepreneurs with desirable startups would do well to assume the standard "rules" are all negotiable.

Every month, entrepreneurs should be able to answer these three questions immediately:

- How much cash do we have?
- How much cash are we burning each month?
- How many months do we have until we run out of money?

Yet, many entrepreneurs I talk to cannot answer these three questions with confidence. Entrepreneurs need to understand the importance of cash and manage it accordingly.

Now that we have our financial story in order, it is time to share our business plan with investors if we cannot afford to bootstrap our own startup funding. There is mystery around this part of the process and that generates anxiety and fear. Your ability to lead t this with confidence is bolstered by the following the process in the previous steps and here again, that should be the outcome of following the process here.

Investment funding comes in the form of equity, debt, seed, and venture funding models. The same principles that we discussed in Customer Identification apply. Investors are customers of our business model. They need to believe in us, our idea, our product, and our ability to execute the business plan. Therefore, we are focused on building an understanding of each type of investment funding and the norms that have been established for securing an investment agreement that supports rather than undermines our business goals.

Starting a business is expensive. Even the simplest business idea requires startup funding. After all, computers and equipment are not free. If we have a business idea that we want to bring to fruition, seeking outside financing is a logical step. There are four levels of financing available during the startup and first years of business. Understanding how to find the right investor at the right business stage is a core capability of an innovation business leader.

Equity – through this form of investment, we agree to give up a share of ownership and profits in return for the investment funds. Money that is invested in a firm by its owner(s) or holder(s) of common stock (ordinary shares) but which is not returned in the normal course of the business. Investors recover it only when they sell their shareholdings to other investors, or when the assets of the firm are liquidated, and proceeds distributed among them after satisfying the firm's obligations. Also called equity contribution.

Equity investors will be looking for the sound basis for our business plan and our exit strategy. This type of funding is most appropriate for a C Corp structure, however other forms can use this if their exit strategy is to sell to another company and they have the equity distribution tied to the forthcoming sale to make distribution.

Debt – this is feasible for low-entry cost ideas and businesses. Businesses whose primary business is conducted online, reducing costs in facilities and locations, provide a service and their prototyping approach focused on packaging relevant services into consumable products fits here. This is usually self-funded by the business leader through securing personal loans to be repaid by the business. These decisions are examples of the types of major decisions and resolutions that must be documented. Wealthy individuals who have their next great idea maybe after a successful exit strategy from a previous business are in a wealth position to use this strategy, however, they frequently select another strategy that reduces their personal liability.

Seed - Seed money is funding collected from investors and used to start a business. For example, if we have developed a new software app and our family or friends invest $10,000 each, that is seed money. Also, if our software is revolutionary, angel investors may take a liking to our product and help us develop and mass produce it. In return for their investments, they own a percentage of our business. Later, when the business is up and running and turning a profit, we can pay them back, or they can sell their stakes to others who are looking for startup investment opportunities.

Early Stage - Your software app has been fully developed and is being produced and shipped to customers. Now we want to expand by adding employees or streamlining our production. Even if we are turning a profit, it may not be enough to cover the costs of daily operations and the expansion. Early-stage financing comes in two parts. Series A financing generates more funding than seed funding, but the risks are higher. Venture capitalists are most likely to invest in our business at this stage, and the method of raising funds involves allotting preferred stock to investors.

After our company is turning a profit, if additional funding is needed, Series B financing can take place. Series B funding is used to increase production, to execute a marketing plan, and to compete head-on with competitors. During this stage, the criteria for funding is determined by evaluating the profit forecasts, how our company stacks up against its main competition, and whether intellectual property is involved and if so, its value in the marketplace. The funding limits are higher than Series A, but the risks are lower for the investor.

Investment Funding Sources

Now that we have established a common set of language and naming around investment funding, the discussion moves to where we can find investors. Angel investors can be our guardian angel or our worst nightmare. Attracting and selecting the right angel investor takes research. We have developed our business plan and the facts and figures. Now we research what angel investors are out there that we can pitch to, so they buy into our idea and prototype enough to ante up the desired funding. These investors fall into three categories: friends and family, single angel investors, angel investor networks. Let us look through the benefits and pitfalls of each type.

Friends and Family – we are confident business innovation leaders and we are all about learning how to overcome the 1 in 10 odds of business failure for startups. They are attractive in that they know us, and they know our talents and energy for our idea and prototype. They do not have traditional strict lending policies. Yet, there is risk. If they are not prepared to risk 100% of their investment both financially and psychologically, they will be at every family dinner for years to come and /or are our support structure for the highs and lows of this up and down adventure.

If we go down this road, treat them for what they are, angel investors. Show them our pitch, financials, and approach them as we would another category of investor. Sign a contract that specifies all of the risks and rewards for both parties. Go through the contract with them. They may still be upset if the startup fails, but it will not be from failure of disclose or integrity on our part.

Single Angel Investors – the bar is high, and it takes time to build a relationship and credibility if we are an unknown business today. They are hard to find, and they typically have an industry or specialty they focus on as part of their risk-mitigation strategy. There are lists of these investors that we can find on the internet. Do your research, identify local investors who want to promote startups in their own backyard. Follow your industry and customer research and look for investors who specialize in your niche. Start by building a relationship and credibility first. The pitch comes later. These types of investors would rather fund $55 million to an established company than $500K to an unknown startup.

This is where building the relationship and knowing your market, product, and financials sets you apart from the rest of the crowd, who are caught up in the idea without substance behind the request. We may have better success at an introduction by working with an accelerator. We provide the construct and focus on early stage profit and risk minimization, which can make the difference. Just to be clear, an accelerator is not a guarantee of funding. It maximizes the potential of the business, but only you and your customer can control the outcome.

Angel Investor Networks - This category is my favorite category: networks aggregating angel investors. Investors set aside funds for angel investments. They set up a screening process by a professional team that sources deals for the network. They benefit by keeping the anonymity of the individual angels. They also have the comfort of a team of smart managers doing due diligence on investment targets on their behalf. We will pitch to their manager. That network and manager have a defined set of criteria by interest and location, similar to the individual angel. They benefit in the scale of the deals they can find as a network versus individual funding. Instead of one angel investing $1M by themselves, 100 angels aggregate $100M and invest as a group in the deals they like the best, individually or collectively. And, on the flipside, it is much easier for us to raise our full amount needed with one phone call, instead of calling the investors individually. The process can be quicker this way.

From my experience, I have noticed that intimidation and anxiety about what investors want is the biggest hurdle. Overanalyzing the facts, figures, and the best investor type or resource can lead to a critical loss of momentum at this phase. We want some level of flexibility and feedback from the investor. Your goal is not to have the perfect, textbook set of documents. Your goal is to authentically represent your idea, your product and your experience in the best light and ask for help. Once you have the case together, it is a numbers game. Not numbers in the sense of funding, but in the sense of making enough connections and outreach to find the investor that believes in you and your work.

Implement a Pilot Launch of your Product and Business

Implementation of a pilot market launch is ideal. If we can create a beta product launch with the appropriate discount and mechanisms for feedback, we will iterate the bugs and kinks out of our software or business. Restaurants often do a soft launch inviting the families of their employees in to serve their menu. They get feedback from the experience as well as the guests on the quality of the food, menu options, service, atmosphere, etc. They can get comfortable before their actual launch to scale and identify any gaps with a safe audience.

Key components of a pilot market launch are; finalize your roll-out strategy, define your test implementation success metrics, run the pilot launch, measure prototype launch effectiveness, determine spin in or spin out strategy for product (going concerns), then finally define the roadmap to product production and formal market entry.

Roll-out strategy finalized – these are the questions we need to build a project plan for the pilot. What are the dates and duration of the pilot, who is the focus group for the pilot? It may be a subset of our avatar client profile or a group of investors, friends, and family. There may be a production test involved to build a small product inventory and test how the product is manufactured and distributed to a single location.

Define test implementation success metrics – this should be a test of our long-term metrics that we will monitor after the broader market launch. For a small population focus on quantitative metrics with some qualitative feedback captured via an anonymous survey. Respondents are more candid when the feedback is anonymous. This will test our reporting for operational effectiveness and customer service feedback mechanisms in addition to providing not only visibility of the success of the pilot, but also determining if the information we are collecting will serve us in the long run.

Run pilot launch – execute the launch as designed. Revenue is collected, production is executed, customers are solicited for their feedback, just as we designed in our business model, but on a limited scale.

Measure prototype launch effectiveness – introspection, reason, and intuition are the key capabilities we will employ in reviewing the reports and survey feedback. Managing by walking around is essential to view all aspects of the business and gain feedback from our team.

Determine spin-in or spin-out strategy for product – based on the launch metrics, the final decision will be made as to whether this product stays in house or becomes a spin-off company.

Define roadmap to product production and formal market entry – this specifies if the results warrant an immediate rollout, any changes to the product, and the timing for official launch as a result of the findings and analysis.

The goal is not long extensive plans but a clear understanding of what the pilot will encompass, how long it will run, an objective assessment of the pilot and how to adapt, if needed, our market entry to create the conditions for success.

CHAPTER THREE
EXTEND

Extend the Business Model

We see in the introductory picture play is something that should not be set aside just because we are considered adults. If you walk inside of most major technology companies you will see areas that are set aside for different types of play. There may be a ping pong table or gaming stations in one area that encourage joint, interactive play. Other areas are quiet areas when people can look inward and look at other activities to activate their imagination and get curious about what the next generation of products, services or even the company may look like.

Curiosity is a state of openness that something might not be what you perceive it to be. It is being open to hearing others' ideas and viewpoints. If we are not curious— if we are only thinking about our own company, our own team, our own work, and our own thoughts and opinions — we spend a whole lot of time never really caring about anyone or anything else.

Creating the whole system model, as we did in Chapter 3, Emerge, serves to provide a holistic point of view, yet, it cannot become shelf-ware that was done once and filed as complete. It should be posted somewhere prominent in your work area and you may want to add a review to a periodic meeting to review, refresh, and keep current. It can be used to ground you, initiate interest, and stimulate curiosity on your perspective when you walk potential vendors, employees, and customers through your point of view. In this chapter, it serves as a catalyst to understand all aspects of the business model we are designing and how each part relates to the other for workflow and communications.

Exponential growth requires an extensible framework to handle not just iterative or continuous improvement, but to propel the business forward. In the second chapter we explored the process for taking an idea all the way through to implementing the new product or service into your business. Now we will extend our perspective to broaden it and look at the business as a whole. The idea is a part of your business, yet your vision and mission are likely much bigger than one product. Now we will delve into what it takes to build a business framework that can support the entire business.

Let us look at Crocs. They came out with a product that met the needs of a broad customer base. Then they reached market saturation because everyone who wanted it already had it. Their first attempt was expansion, they added colors and sizes to reach their client base to buy more of a similar product. This worked for a while, but to really be a viable business, they had to extend their product line with new styles and features to appeal to a new audience. This process required new production, marketing, and other support structures to extend the company's reach.

We need to see the future of the business as an entire picture to build a framework that can be extended by taking the initiative to extend the viability of the business, developing the intention, and feeling confident to extend that reach given the discerning the conditions and risks that are to be respected in deciding not to extend.

Highly Calibrated "Why" Questions

The four dimensions of a full spectrum life are your vision and your "why". For each of us we try to compartmentalize business and philanthropy, health and wellness, relationships and love and time and money freedom into separate buckets. This is a great construct for writing or teaching, yet our day-to-day lives are often a whirlwind where they are becoming inextricably merged together. How do we lead through the chaos of the whirlwind to achieve what is most important and not necessarily the most urgent? It is returning to our center, our why as a guidepost in how we answer all of the rest of the what, where, who, and how questions that become our business model. It is the fulcrum of the seesaw image in value drivers that helps us find the balance, the tipping point or other driver we seek to pull all of the pieces of the puzzle together.

For solopreneurs, the individual is the business and the concept that easily resonates. We know that we are designing a business model that not only serves the customer's needs, but also requires us to decide how big and how far we want to extend our vision in business while still honoring the other three dimensions of our lives.

For small businesses, you have a large pool of staff that can assist you in delegation of tasks that are routine or not your sweet spot for adding value. This frees up time for the other dimensions yet adds some complexity in leadership of your team behind your mission.

For larger businesses, you may not be the CEO/President, but you may be a valued member of the senior leadership team guiding the vision of the owner of the business in that dimension, but needing to set boundaries and manage your time and effectiveness is vital to not crowd the other dimensions of your life. Your goal as the business leader in this context is to fully understand the organization vision and mission and to lead your staff in achieving their goals, but also to work in concert with the other leaders to achieve the organization's goal.

Regardless of what size organization you are leading or your role, having a full spectrum vision of your why helps you rise personally as a business leader over the constant barrage of delays, distractions, and temptation so you can be pragmatic instead of charting a course and using your internal GPS system to follow your why.

Highly Calibrated "What" Questions

We will take a deeper look at each of the questions posed in the first chapter to look at how we approach innovation leadership for designing the business model framework.

Product Strategy

In the second chapter we focused on what it takes to bring a new product to market. The objective of a framework is to understand how each product contributes to the overall company strategy. For a small business, it is easy to be focused on the first product and not look forward 2 – 5 years to forecast customer needs and problems that we can solve. The software app that we developed in an earlier example is now on the market. The vision needs to be extended by asking questions and doing the research on other apps that have the same avatar customer is one path we can follow. Another is exploring how to extend the reach of the additional app by mining the analytics we capture for metrics.

An example is a software that is designed to solve or significantly modify a societal problem. The initial product may be designed for one group of users. Prescribing physicians have the opportunity to accelerate access to insurance companies and contractors after a natural disaster by supplying all information in a single application that is transmitted in near time to insurance companies, a contractor connection business, and state databases to prevent contractor price gouging. However, by adding another software that leverages artificial intelligence, it can take the data collected in the first software and extend the benefit by modeling the demographics, damage reported, and other demographics to identify patterns that can help insurance companies to find alternative resettlement locations when weather patterns indicate that the build or damage rebuild cycle is unsustainable. Then we can look at other classes of disasters as market opportunities. Another opportunity is linking the state databases to prevent bad contractors from crossing state lines to avoid detection in the chaos that follows a natural disaster.

Business Strategy

Continuing on to business strategy with the software example, the first application may be developed in one software to feature security, speed, and anonymization of data. However, Artificial Intelligence is required for the data science capabilities. Understanding what technology should be used, the timing and creation the staff or contractors to support the development of the business rules, consumer usability and the various requirements and regulations does not happen overnight. The vision and strategy are the guideposts of the R&D, human resources, technology, and marketing needed to support a complex but industry-altering technology.

We can easily see the similarities in the image of the value chain and the three-dimensional Slinky® toy.

Actually, when holding a Slinky® toy in our hands, we can see that as we stretch in one area, it causes a corresponding contraction in another. We have four different points of view that align to create the synergy for a successful business venture.

Situational leadership requires mastering the balance of our unique DNA leadership profile. We demonstrate that through our understanding the concept of applying the value drivers we are developing requires understanding the value levers we will apply in decision-making to understand the trade-offs we make in either the short-term or long-term when making these decisions. I find that knowledge is power and therefore it is important to build a common understanding about value levers up front.

One set of value levers is Customization vs. Standardization as shown at a remarkably high level in the graphic below. We determine the level of Standardization we want to employ as our business model. This applies regardless if we offer a service or a product. The methods we use to control the standards will vary whether it is a service or a product as well 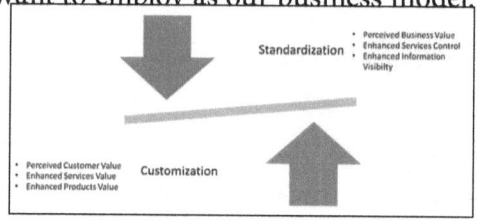 as the complexity, however, the business model requires this decision to be made.

This decision is a prerequisite to defining our end-to-end processes and our organization and delivery decisions. Before we move ahead, 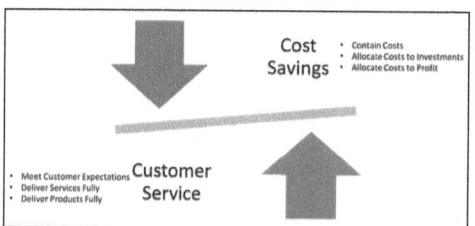 there is another value lever that must also be considered. This value lever is Customer Service vs. Cost Savings. What balance will we be able to strike between these two key aspects of our business model as depicted below?

Our end to end processes and organization strategy are also dependent on our decisions on these value forces.

Standardization – This decision for how we will standardize or customize our services or product will be based on our vision for how we deliver our unique value to our target customer. Did we highlight that we have unlocked the best way to do something? Then we will choose a standardized model that maintains the quality of that unique differentiator. If our answer was that we listen to what is different about each customer and tailor our solution to match their needs, then we will select a highly customized business model. This in turn has an impact on our pricing and anticipated volume. We need to be aware of these impacts as we design our end-to-end process models to be able to manage the differences that are required.

End-to-End Processes – for a standardized process we can introduce automation and repetition for consistency and quality control. This has the advantage of managing the higher anticipated volume. It may require a higher upfront investment, yet is likely to yield a strong ROI, which should be a metric we can measure. For highly-customized business models, the opposite approach is recommended, meaning we would add more service or product variations and a catalog of the variations and significant investment into the development of all personnel who have client interactions to create a personalized experience. This investment is steady throughout and is reflected in a lower volume higher price per transaction model.

Outsourcing Strategy – for a standardized process business model this is a more viable option. For a high-customization business model, a business alliance strategy is preferable. We would create a referral strategy with complimentary high-touch businesses that create a network. For example, my hair salon does not offer nails, massages, or other similar services so they work with a nearby wellness center to refer them for massages, and the nearby nail salon for those services, in return, they refer their customers to her for hair services they don't provide.

Digital – for online businesses this is the heart of our business. Think back to our avatar client, we learn where they hang out. Then we determine if we will have a presence there too. When we decide to develop that presence, we decide whether we make transactions or if we just hang around there with the hopes of set up a conversation for a bigger sale. We adopt their perspective when we analyze how easy or hard, we make it for them to buy from us. If the screen takes more than three seconds to load, we have lost them, no matter how great whatever was coming was going to be. We have the foresight to make sure our digital strategy is optimized for mobile recognizing because fewer customers sit at a desktop computer than before.

Brick and mortar businesses also need to understand what they are buying to form their digital strategy. Here is how an entrepreneur who is a Puerto Rican expert baker attracts his tribe. He is on Facebook live every day and his recording is done in the front of the café. By being in the mix, he is showcasing his food, his busy bakery, his customers not only enjoying his food but the lively atmosphere of being there and creating the experience in the minds of the viewers of his video. What is the result? Puerto Ricans come from neighboring states on Saturdays because they want to be a part of that. Another opportunity was generated when a local luxury hotel came to ask him to bake the bread for their hotel and other businesses use his bakery for their videos because it is a fun destination. It not only improves his bottom-line, but it also creates the demand for the culture and community he loves. Seeing him talk about his bakery like that, it was evident that his tribe was just as important as the financial benefits he is accruing.

Metrics – Measuring all aspects of the business is important. Financials, customer service, inventory, sales calls, and conversions are obvious quantitative measures. It is also important to honor and measure the qualitative aspects as well. There are quantitative metrics that can be employed, measures that help us track if we are taking the right actions to keep us on course, which are called lead measures. They measure activity that may be in the number of product designs, sales calls, marketing spend by channel, development cost to budget, vendor contracts submitted, prototypes completed, and quality defect reviews completed.

Lag measures are for results or outcomes when these measure sales closed, the vendor contracts signed, the accounts receivables collected, product designs finalized, and the products have been released from design to production. Other key measures are customer service calls, time to resolution, and number of escalations per caller.

An opportunity to manage this lever is to align the metrics with the goals of the model. Selecting metrics that are suitable for a standardized business model when adopting a customized business model will result in organizational tension and drama as the metrics are out of alignment with the desired performance behaviors.

Avatar Client

There are three opportunities that each have different avatar client in this example. The first product is targeted at the consumer to simplify the report filing and recovery from the damage. The second is to aggregate the data for government agencies and insurance companies to look at their future forecasting. The third is back to a consumer, for a different demographic but with same benefit, and the fourth opportunity requires collaboration with state government to monetize and productize the data collected to consumers and insurance companies to reduce fraud.

Each of the avatars has a different story of varying complexity and depth related to the problem they are addressing. The consumer may be in shock and overwhelmed from the disaster yet required to complete a myriad of forms and gather data that may have been damaged in the very storm they are experiencing. They also have anxiety about fairness from insurance companies and the government in providing full settlements in a timely manner.

The insurance company is mobilizing for volume and concerned about claim size and validity from consumers. They also have a set of vetted contractors they work with for routine volume of claims that may not have the capacity to handle a large-scale disaster. They are concerned about public perception, responsiveness, and mitigating damage to reduce claim size.

The government is focused on public perception of their responsiveness, appropriation of the necessary funds to repair infrastructure, and non-consumer owned damage. They are also concerned about the long-term viability of the community at various levels of government and across a variety of agencies.

Contractors are not a direct purchaser of the product; however, their business will be impacted by the introduction of the software suite of products. Understanding their story and interests has the potential to mitigate resistance to adoption by the other stakeholders and a communication and marketing strategy on the benefits to contractors is beneficial.

For each of these avatars we determine the problem they are trying to solve and identify their most basic need for survival. It is vital that our message is relevant to their survival. Boil it down to the primitive desires to be safe, healthy, happy, and strong. Keywords that are great to incorporate for businesses making a social impact are conserving resources, conserving time, building networks, gaining influence for our cause to be taken seriously, accumulating resources, innate desire to be generous, and desire for meaning and purpose.

As you build the avatar, you may identify other avatar customers, product features, and new ideas to be stored in a database to sequence and fold into the business strategy.

Brand Strategy

Now that we have identified their problem, they need to see us as their guide. How does our service or product solve their need? When defining the value, we need to present them with the heart of our message, and we have already started down that path. So, take the next step and show them the plan we have in mind as their guide. Open the curtains, let the sunshine in, and help them understand that we really understand how to guide them down the path to their destination, not just a generic destination. As you build trust with your capabilities to develop the right plan, we ask them to decide and act. Without that step we have laid out a plan, but we have not converted a sale. The next step, which is frequently overlooked, is to describe the cost of inaction to our avatar client. We remind them that staying in their current position is more costly than the cost of joining us in serving our cause by buying our product is the key to ending in a successful outcome.

Highly Calibrated "Where" Questions

This is about building your long-term strategy in phases. For early startups they may choose to work from a home office to redirect investment dollars to other costs. Yet, to extend and grow, most businesses will need facilities to support their growth. Product manufacturing, warehousing, and professional meeting spaces are examples of spaces that may start out with an initial launch approach and be extended over time into contracted/leased facilities and potentially into self-developed facilities over time. Failure to use your ideation and innovation skills on location can result in disruption and loss of reputation and business, if not planned out, as this is rarely a quick process.

Location Requirements

Location is more than online and offline for customer sales. Decisions are needed on the location of where your product will be manufactured. If the manufacturing process is a trade secret, we may decide to produce the product in-house. If not, contracting with an existing manufacturer with excess capacity is a better option. This strategy can also be part of your exit strategy, if that company becomes proficient in the process and wants to buy out your company at a future date.

Selecting the location depends on the need for customer access and visibility, square footage, and in the case of a business designed to extend, ability to lease (build or build out) adjacent space as your company grows. Sure, moving is an option, yet it can be costly beyond the actual space requirements. There are also the considerations for all of your marketing materials to be updated with the new information and a specific campaign to ease the transition. Another cost is in lost business when you are inviting customers in. They do not read the address change materials, GPS software does not quickly adapt to your new location, and the environment and ambiance of the place can be changed significantly with a move.

Location Review

Value drivers come into play here. The potential space may fit your budget but not your purpose and mission. Or vice versa, you found the ideal space and now need to seek more investment to cover and adjust your business case and model. Here is where seeking advice from a local real estate expert can make a huge difference in the long-term success of the venture. Beyond the available space, determine what owner build out (floorplan) restrictions (does the landlord allow certain grease filters required for French fries if you are making in a restaurant, the correct venting for a dry cleaner, build out (cutting through an exterior wall) for drive up window, dressing rooms for a clothes store, security for a high value retail location, etc.), if any, are part of the package.

Identify any additional benefits that offset a cost difference. Access to dry cleaners, childcare, building-wide cafeterias, and restaurants can save time and provide networking opportunities. Along that same line of thought, look at the list of other tenants. Do they have a business that would negate or enhance your business? It is interesting but not well-known fact that a shoe store is more successful in a location that is near other shoe stores. We see that with car dealerships as well. Your customer wants to reduce their hassle of driving around town and confine their search to a set area. Being in that range is a great value.

Safety is a huge consideration. I worked for a company doing surprise on-site operational audits. One location was across the street from a crack house and while I was appalled at the shoot-out while coming to visit, I cannot imagine how it was to come to that area every day for work and how they attracted and retained quality talent in that environment. While that is an extreme example, a well-lit parking, property owner security, and customer perception also play a key role in selecting a location.

Location Regulations

Working with a real estate expert helps give you an edge when it comes to zoning restrictions and understanding the growth or contraction trajectory of the location. Up and coming areas may offer incentives for new businesses such as tax credits and rent reductions.

There may be restrictions for emissions from your manufacturing process as well as basic restrictions and regulations at play. Some business types cannot be located near school, others near a church. Some locations have restrictions on liquor sales on Sundays, which affects restaurants and bars.

Metrics and Reporting

To extend, your metrics and accountability reporting should be designed to provide the data you need to determine the breakeven point between contracting and in-house, as well when to change out a piece of the business relationship ecosystem you are building. Contracts should have defined performance requirements and deliverables to guide the analysis. Timeliness, quality, and other considerations vary by the type of contracted service and the criticality to your mission and purpose.

For startups that are still in the innovation launch process, taking advantage of the government tax requirements for corporate veil and the Augusta rule can create a win/win situation. We fulfill the mandatory monthly meeting requirements and put these questions on the table from a strategic perspective. Review of progress made this month, determining if am we are ahead of the curve or behind the curve in our business plan; identifying new actions we can take today to propel our idea, our product incubation, our investment sourcing, or day-to-day operations forward are all topics for the meeting.

Key actions and specific supporting details that should be kept in each month's meeting are change of location, changes in corporation membership, and officer changes. Financial minutes should address new loans made and the details and money borrowed and details. Additional facilities in form of lease or purchase include vehicle lease purchase agreements, new joint ventures, partnerships or franchises, extension into additional states, DBA agreements, contracts over an amount specified in your resolutions, change in tax status, employee benefit offerings, changes in banking arrangements, payroll service or company, accountant or attorney changes, and changes in designated salary.

Resolutions are also documented monthly as needed, travel expense authorization, seminars, education and training, cell phone, website provider, bonus ceiling amounts, new hires, independent contractors, advertising budget, donation limits, entertainment, credit cards secured, general purchase ceiling amount, merchant account, and petty cash.

Highly Calibrated "Who" Questions

Similarly, to the concept in the "How" questions if we get bogged down with concerns over power, influence, and names. Reframe the question to a "What" question instead. Instead of asking yourself "Who" needs to do this, reframe it into "What" capabilities are required. Early in my career I was an accountant, so I know the basics, but I do not study each change to the tax code, so a CPA looks at my financial records and does my taxes. I know enough to make sure that I set up my financial records appropriately, and I am not defrauded, but I know what my limits are and take the appropriate actions to delegate those actions to focus my attention where I can make the most difference. As my business grows, leveraging a bookkeeping service is planned to enable greater capacity. As leaders we review our organization's capacity and capabilities. It does not matter whether we are in the launch, going concern, or scaling stage of maturity, we still must review on a periodic basis as a best practice with reviews from a different perspective as key performance indicators are measured for trigger points.

Leaders who want to make an impact must have a team. We choose our teams. We choose the organization we work for, if we are not self-employed and we mentor, grow, hire, and terminate the people within our direct teams. We also choose who we collaborate with across the organization to make our end-to-end processes flow well. As business owners, we are responsible for choosing our teams, some come on board as employees and advisors as the company grows and expands. Others come on board via contracts and other modalities.

To achieve your vision, here are examples of who you can enlist to be part of your team given the appropriate agreements: Bookkeeper, CPA, Tax Strategist, Financial Advisor, Virtual Assistant, Office Manager, Payroll service provider, insurance brokers, commercial real estate brokers, investors, a Board of Directors, leaders of local community charities, Chamber of Commerce, supply chain vendors, shipping and receiving, and customer service. Just because our payroll is small does not mean that these and other key services vendors and partners are not a significant part of your success strategy.

Returning to the concept of value drivers, for founders of small businesses, the individual is the business and the drivers for value are capabilities and time. When you apply more time, you can learn and grow into the capabilities above, even if you don't have them as you start your business, because these are all skills that can be learned through a variety of media available at hand through the internet and books like this. What is not expandable is time. You make tradeoffs each day on where you can add the most value. Are you adding more value learning skills or is it more valuable to leverage the skills you have to hire the skills to fill the gap? Beyond that tradeoff, is back to your why, your vision and purpose for doing this venture.

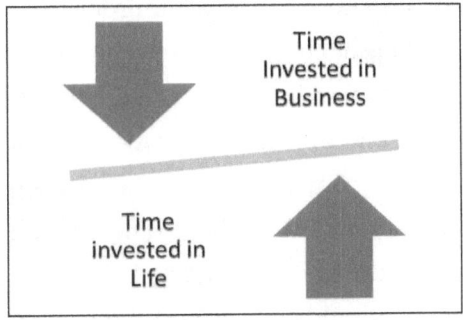

Your other dimensions in your life demand time too. Are you building a legacy for your family and ignoring them in the process of building that legacy? Are you committed to the cause you are serving and delaying the benefit to the cause by taking longer to reach the potential of the business to create a bigger impact? Here is an example of the value driver tradeoffs. The key to wealth and value creation is moving away from this persistent trade of of time for money, it is learning how to create income from multiple streams and the power of delegation to move from simple math of 5+5 =10 to advanced math where $5^2=25$. Changing the paradigm is the difference between comfort and wealth.

Governance Structure – As a leader of a small organization in terms of headcount we may be wearing many hats. Our intuition can help us discern if those hats fit equally well. We may need to add the right subject matter and leadership resources to fit our business vision. Is the organization matrixed, traditional, or a set of relationships? An organization chart is the most frequently used device for tracking internal governance. This same concept can be used and color-coded for outsourced relationships.

Customer Communications – everyone who works in a business is customer service. However, not everyone has the same perspective, capabilities, and talents. Are our people empowered to solve the problem at-hand and then communicate what was done or do they only have authority and responsibility up to a certain point before it needs to be escalated? In the fast-paced world of social media and online communications, it is critical that whoever is responsible for communications has a deep connection with our brand, our customers, and the ability to cut through the emotion and complexity to work out the right statement.

Organization Design – This concept should be viewed as larger than the traditional organization chart. It builds on that and informs our culture, values, job role descriptions for recruiters, succession planning, career development, retention, compensation, and benefits. We often this in terms of an organization chart. While that is a necessary component of good organization design, it is not the whole design.

Board of Directors - There are a number of areas where directors can help their portfolio companies be successful. Legally, directors are required to provide governance and oversight, however the directors of an early-stage company may choose to be more proactive by adding a great deal of business value and advice. No director is able to provide value in all areas, but great directors often help where they can and make introductions to the right resources when they cannot.

Recruiting - is one of the most important ways in which directors can help. Companies are only as good as the collection of entrepreneurs that populate them. It really matters who you are able to recruit. In an industry where nothing matters more than the people, helping bring in the absolute best people should be a top priority for all directors.

Fundraising— Making sure that a company does not run out of funds is a key part of the early stage director's job. Fundraising can occupy a CEO full time and is to the detriment of spending time growing the business. Working with the CEO to hone the investment pitch and introducing potential investors are especially important director assignments.

Strategic Advice— Active seed investors can serve as directors and leverage their access to a wide range of experiences both from the standpoint of being former/current entrepreneurs and being investors. They are deeply involved in the startup ecosystem and do not spend their days focused on only one company. Many CEOs get lost in the weeds of their company's day-to-day operations. We need someone with a broader world view who can provide both a sounding board and strategic direction. However, a good director does not micro-manage the business; it is the CEO's job to run the company.

Making Connections and Finding/Attracting Initial Customers— One advantage to be a member of a large angel group is the strength of their network. For example, Launchpad members have access to literally thousands of potential partners, investors, analysts, customers, service providers, and employees through their network. Making connections through networks like these will prove invaluable to a company.

Save Time— Directors can help companies avoid spinning their wheels. Startups all have to find an office, set up payroll, manage their finances, etc. As angel investors, we have connections to the service providers that handle these mundane but essential tasks.

Risk Management— It is the director's responsibility to ensure that the controls in place are appropriate for each stage of development. Investor directors participate in regular communication with financial/accounting advisors, should have confidence in those advisors, and should review and discuss stage-appropriate controls on a regular basis.

Evaluating the CEO— Directors have a responsibility to ensure that we as the CEO are up to the task. Where there are concerns, the involved board tries to help develop their CEO. Studies show that founder CEOs generally outperform external candidates because of their burning desire and vision. Sometimes it becomes clear that the current CEO objectively cannot do the job, so the directors must initiate the process of replacing him/her. Objectivity is important – a CEO should be judged on whether they are effective, not whether their style is the same as the directors who are evaluating them. When replacing a CEO, key traps to avoid failing to determine what kind of CEO is needed include rushing the process, mistaking charisma for skill, under-estimating the experience value of past failure, and failure to do deep, blind. and thorough reference and background checking.

Ensuring a Successful Exit— Directors have a fiduciary responsibility to maximize value for shareholders. Investors invest in startup companies with the promise of eventual liquidity for their otherwise illiquid stock, and the expectation of many shareholders is that the company will achieve an exit by sale of the company in a reasonable time frame. Directors need to make sure that the management team understands the path to an exit that provides maximum returns to all shareholders. Directors should regularly focus on this issue, making sure the process is understood, the level of preparedness is adequate, and the requisite experience is represented at the board or company level. In my mind this function resembles the function of a scorer and attester in professional golf. Reviewing the score presented and signed for by the players counterpart of the day protects the entire golf field of players from inaccurate scoring.

Leadership Team – at this point you are even more aware of the variety of capabilities and behaviors, not to mention time that is dedicated to launching a startup technology business with a social impact mission. It makes sense to apply the principles in the roles of the director to our role as business leader in attracting, recruiting, and onboarding a committed leadership team that is aligned around the business vision and mission.

Decision Authority - Decision rights, authority, and escalation can be mapped out and documented. This can lead to challenges. For example, the fear of deciding because the person does not understand if it is their role, so they delegate upwards. The opposite can also happen, if clear boundaries and values are documented, two different people can be making conflicting decisions and create confusion. This is important as you create your Board of Directors as noted above.

Talent Capabilities – Evaluation of talent and performance is an art and a science. Once we have created the governance structure and organization design, here is where the decisions on recruiting, application process, and interviews begin. Attracting and selecting the right talent is essential for any business. There are the scientific type evaluation metrics, do they meet the essential job role requirements? What is their level of education and experience and is it a match to the job role? The art is in the identification of the intangible qualities that will make the applicant the best candidate, does their attitude and personality fit with the vision we have painted?

Training and Development – Retention of talent is typically cheaper than replacement, yet a bad hire is just that. How do we structure the job performance measures and reviews to give appropriate, actionable feedback that helps our organization grow? Are we in a business that requires ongoing certification for professional development and/or regulatory compliance? If so, how do we structure the training access? Is that outsourced by the employee and reimbursed pending successful completion or is it self-funded by the employee?

Highly Calibrated "When" Questions

Establishing the metrics and governance structure we have reviewed provides the data you need to make an informed decision on the viability of the proposed extension you are envisioning. It extends your perspective beyond the new cool idea, business partnership proposal, or new service or technology that has the potential to extend your business to a focus on your overall business model, and if it is designed, to support the proposal.

Those are all based on conditions and situations in your business. Our challenge as entrepreneurs and business leaders is to create the vision and culture of rising above the conditions and situations to achieve our mission. To accomplish this, we establish the picture of success in our minds. It becomes reality when and only when our belief in the vision aligns with the actions we have taken were in alignment with the opportunity for success.

On any given day opportunity presents itself. It may present itself as an angry customer who tells you exactly where your product defect is in no uncertain terms. We may not be ready to hear that information on that day, yet if we have someone on our staff who is great at calming the customer down and getting past the noise of their complaint, we may recognize on that day or on another day, after other similar, if less boisterous complaints come in, that a pattern is in fact emerging and we should pay attention. When we come into alignment with that feedback and take the right actions, we can turn the tide and chart a course for customer satisfaction, instead of frustration.

CHAPTER FOUR
EXPAND

Controlled Expansion Leveraging Curiosity as our Focus

The Slinky® toy line expanded and one element beyond colors and materials was the addition of the Slinky Dog®. We may choose to expand in both expected and unexpected directions, over time.

As exponential business leaders, we cannot underestimate what curiosity does for us and our teams. In a Harvard Business Review survey of 3,000 workers in China, Germany, and the United States, 84% of respondents noted a belief that curiosity catalyzes new ideas; 74% said it inspires unique, valuable talents; and, 63% of them voiced that being curious helps you get promoted. The study also points to the fact that curiosity also does the following:

Creates more open communication and better team performance - Curious people are open to hearing one another's thoughts. It makes sense that their teams perform better because they actually want to hear what their teammates have to say.

Reduces group conflict - By being open to others, curious people are not afraid of what others say and think. Hard conversations do not turn them off. Instead, curious people ask even more questions and tend to be open to disagreement because they know they will learn something from it—at the very least, how to relate better to the people around them.

Encourages more innovation and promotes positive changes in both creative and noncreative jobs - If people are questioning the status quo and feel empowered to do so, they are much more open to finding new ways of doing things, leading people to enjoy their work more, no matter what role they're in.

Reduces decision-making errors -This is one of my favorites. It is a bit counterintuitive, but the more open you are to try and experiment (and therefore, the more you are open to possible failure), the faster you learn. When you believe your way of doing things is right all the time, you do not stop and ask if what you are doing is actually the best way to do something. Which means being curious actually makes us fundamentally better at our jobs, as we test and iterate on our processes, our programs, and truly everything else.

Improves your sales techniques - And, this one was not part of the research study, but I believe it to be absolutely true. Curious salespeople and account managers generate more revenue for a company. Why? They actually care about the client they are talking to rather than just pushing a product down someone's throat. They want to hear the struggles on the other side of the table, and they ask what clients are actually looking for, instead of being laser-focused on what they are already offering.

How We Can All Be More Curious - Believe in the business case of cultivating curiosity. If we are not naturally curious, which a lot of us were not raised or trained to be, it can help to believe that there truly is a business case to being curious. Check out the research cited above if you want more data on it. Read some business books on curiosity and innovation—two intimately linked concepts—and study companies you believe embody curiosity. I genuinely think a foundational belief in the value of curiosity is essential to care about incorporating it into our business and life practices.

Start with "why" and ask it a lot - In almost every discussion, we can do the "Five Why" test. It seems like something only your three-year-old does when you tell them not to do something, but the goal is actually to get at the deeper thing driving your thoughts, ideas, or behaviors. And, when we see what is really driving us, we get so much more clarity around whether we are on the right track, what our real motivations are, or whether something needs to shift. It is also a great technique for conversation starters at networking events, conventions, etc. where we are meeting new people because our curiosity invites them to open up and create a stronger and more memorable interaction that has the potential to grow our businesses through the higher quality information we gather and the trust that genuine curiosity creates by demonstrating interest.

Model it for one another - We as business leaders do not have to share our perspective verbally from a soapbox. When we model inquisitiveness and invite one another to think in a way that is more curious, the better we will all be. And, the better our businesses will be in the long run as we establish the work culture we desire.

Curiosity is what fascinates us about the business vision. We can hold firm to the vision while allowing it to expand and evolve by seeing it done, but not being tied to the outcome of any given conversation or task in the plan. Leadership in all its forms employs a mindset component. We learn to focus on leveraging our curiosity to fuel our imagination. Staying in touch with curiosity and imagination allow us to keep expanding our vision for who we want to be as leaders. We choose to honor the pull to growth to cultivate the agility and flexibility in our health and wellness that sustains the leadership mindset required to be maintained throughout our lives and the lifecycle of our business.

There is a powerful mental faculty that we all possess but do not necessarily supported through our educational system. It is applied imagination. Together we'll explore neuroscientific principles found in the works of Dr. Joe Dispenza, epigenetics provided by Robert Lamb, and quantum physics provided by Phillip Ball that will be synthesized and distilled by me for how they impact innovation in a social business.

Neuroscience, Epigenetics, and Quantum Physics Principles

When we are between the ages of two and five our brains operate in Theta brain wave development state as our brain moves from the subconscious to conscious mind development, which is a low energetic frequency of 4-8 cycles per second.[1] They are primarily connected to their internal world and live in the abstract and are connected to their imagination. They accept what they are told as real. Nurture has a huge impact on our development at this stage, if we are told we can be anything, we believe it, if we are told we are stupid, we believe that too. The imagination is immensely powerful in this stage of our development. Our diet also has a large impact. If we grow up eating food that is made from scratch and is a balanced diet, our DNA, genes,and cells have a better nutritional baseline for their daily replication than if we are fed convenience foods, fast food, sugar, salt, and other processed snacks.

Around age five or six we move into Alpha brain wave development, which is 8 – 13 cycles per second, and this stage lasts until around the age of eight. The analytical mind begins to form in this age range and children start to draw conclusions about the laws of external life, yet at the same time their inner world is as real as their outer world. At this stage children can pretend well. Ask them to be an animal or a superhero or try anything on for size and they can be whatever we ask, not only for minutes, but for hours on end. For parents, teachers, and grandparents it can be exhausting, and the temptation is to reign that in our capacity to manage our attention span for imagination. This is where we start introducing the concept in children's minds of what is normal behavior, what is common, what is expected behavior, and, subtly or not so in case, our imagination begins to be reined in. We are not always as encouraged to be whatever we want to be anymore. In Alpha state what we are is pure potentiality and we are in a super position to see from all possibilities what is available to us to us.

At this and the Theta stages we make our own reality as we are so intertwined between the subconscious and the conscious mind. The goal of the meditation series Dr Joe Dispenza has created for both self-healing and for corporate innovation relies on regaining this state with fluidity over time through meditation or applied relaxation and cognitive observation techniques.

We move into Beta wave development, which is above 13 cycles per second, around age eight and the frequencies within Beta have three ranges that we will discuss in other areas of the book as they apply. After age 12 the brain closes the connection between the subconscious and conscious minds. As we age, we move within the three sections of Beta frequencies from low – mid and high ranges.

Leveraging our imagination through meditation, exercise, dance, yoga, or any other modality that works for you, reengages our earlier states. The goal for expanding our imagination is to stick with the activity and focus for a minimum of 30 minutes and ideally an hour. One of the key patterns that emerges if we study the difference in behaviors between a billionaire mindset and our own is the focus on blocking out time in our calendar to do this on a weekly basis. The first 20 minutes or so, we remain in our current state of focus and awareness, when trying to generate imaginative opportunities for growth or to work around a perceived obstacle. Then if we stay with it, we get still and listen to our inner knowing, intuition, or spirit depending on your belief tradition. This is where we move closer to the state of pure potentiality and reopen the connection between our conscious and subconscious minds. This stimulates the synaptic connections and breaks the old patterns of thinking that have produced our current results and opens the door to creating new neuronal pathways that elevate our thinking and focus and enable us to generate the breakthrough ideas required to achieve our desired vision.

Record of Success

Another technique for reopening neuronal pathways is to use our mental faculty of memory in the more well-known capacity of backward memory. We are building a record of our successes, so the goal of this exercise is not just to create a list, but to remind ourselves of the entire experience including the range of emotions we felt when we attained the success. For me, the first time I climbed the big willow tree in our backyard was magical. I could feel the progress as I climbed, I knew there was danger, since I went out on my own with no parents for support. When I climbed near to the top, the sight of our house, yard, and neighborhood from that elevated perspective was thrilling. I dreamed of the building as a tree house so that I could be up there longer and move more freely to enjoy the moment. Then there was the excitement and anxiety of coming back down and making the final leap from the lowest branch back down to our yard. This is the type of imagination we hope to cultivate by doing this exercise. It was easier as a child because we do not think of how we will find the money, time, or materials to build the tree house, we just focused on what we wanted.

Think back to the successes we had from birth to 5 6-year-old age range and the dreams that we wanted to fulfill when we were that age, if we can remember what they were. It may be a simple as tying my shoes, climbing a tree, moving from a tricycle to a bike, whatever it is for us as we think back on our successes. The dreams may be a firefighter, teacher, nurse, doctor, pilot, whatever we thought of as our dream at that age.

As we age and our brains take on more different experiences, we can unconsciously make a shift to using our imaginations to generate worry, what if's, and other forms of anxiety and depression that keep us focused in the past or afraid of moving forward. Humans often use our imagination in the form of worry to torture ourselves with what might go wrong. We may have been socialized to be humble or not shown how to accept praise and compliments with grace and have the mistaken notion that to recognize a pattern of success is bragging or overbearing. We remember best the facts and experiences that have an emotional component. People can have negative associations with those memories. We remember when we did something embarrassing because of the shame we felt. We remember when someone made us angry, but not always when someone did something nice.

As we move to the next age group from 8-12, as our world expands through school and other social affiliations, try to take note of any differences in our successes or experiences between the ages of five and eight that we can recall, if any.

During this period, we are growing rapidly mentally, physically, and there is no such concept of repeating the same experiences from year to year. We are propelled forward by an inner force of growth and do not even consciously consider the rapid changes we have undergone.

The next age range to capture your successes and dreams is in the age range of 12 – 21. Many of us feel the accelerated growth in all dimensions of our life here, and some begin to formulate the patterns of narrowing their potentiality as they begin to focus more on circumstances and barriers rather than remaining focused on ways to make our dreams come true.

The goal of this next range is to acknowledge our successes as alignment with our intelligent growth by design during the ages of 22-40. If we have not let ourselves fully experience the gratitude and joy for these successes, there is not an emotion attached to them. As we recall these successes, we should allow ourselves to feel the joy, gratitude, and other powerful positive emotions that come with the recollection. Then as the emotion fades, step into the analytical and intuitive faculties and identify the patterns that emerge.

We as business leaders and founders are often set apart from our peers at this point. We see that some of our friends and family have made decisions that did not work out or that they regret. Some rise above and demonstrate the resiliency and expansion to redirect their focus back on their vision and goals, others become a weight or drag in our lives and slip down the evolutionary scale to see themselves as victims, rather than as co-creators in designing a life they love. Take an image of an unexpanded Slinky®.

To me, each band of the Slinky® represents living the same life over and over again every year. Do you know a friend or relative that maybe you see at the holidays once a year or every few years and after about 15 minutes they have very little to say, it is because they have very little change in their life. The drive the same route to work, their kids go to the same school, they go to the same church, they have the same job, wear their hair in the same time and essentially live their life the same way in the same pattern, year after year and they aren't living a new year, they are living the same year over 5, 10 or more times. When we repeat the same year multiple times, it acts like an unexpanded life that becomes more rigid and fixed. Some people refer to this as our comfort zone because it is comforting to be in a familiar place. What happens is that we are living the same life 25, 50, 80 times, instead of living a new life each year.

Our comfort zone acts as a traditional spring; it takes on the compression and cushions us from the some of the conditions and situations we face. We built our comfort zones as a pattern of behavior that served us well. Yet springs wear out, they lose their ability to provide that support, and our work to expand is an internal force that leverages our imagination to connect with infinite intelligence and identify what we love, not what we are used to having and most importantly being. One approach to reactivating a past record of success and applying it to today's circumstances and situations is to conduct a review. This image reminds me of the expanded Slinky® and how it correlates to the growth curve.

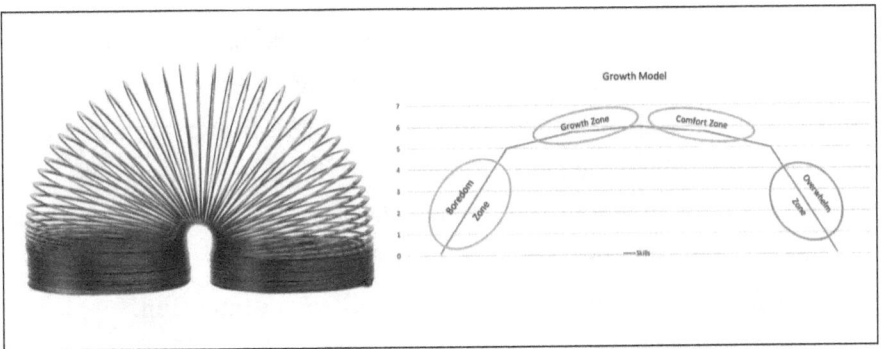

When it is expanded, we see space between the rings, and it is no longer circular but rather a spiral as the pull to growth is exerted. When we introduce pace and growth into our lives, we elevate our thinking and therefore our potential

The next portion of this exercise will take a varying amount of time based on our age and experience from 41 – present. This is important. First, we may see patterns emerge that we never noticed before, particularly if we have never done this exercise. This is not, I repeat, not a CV or resume exercise. Career highlights may emerge, but it is also other types of successes such as finding the love of our life, taking a fabulous trip, volunteering for a cause, competing the 3-day Ironman Triathlon, whatever it is. For our dreams, maybe there was always a pattern there, but it is now seeking to reveal itself and writing down a success that is not a part of the work quadrant of our lives may hold the key to unlocking the pattern of what we view as success and what we truly value.

What is revealing itself is the pattern of our expanded capabilities as we experienced life. We know that our history does not define us. Yet building that record of success is a powerful tool in our arsenal for facing the future. We have built a mental library of pictures and emotions to call upon. When we are tempted to indulge in self-torture instead of self-leadership, we can now flip our perspective to real successes and use those as leverage to build a strong foundation for future success, instead of focusing on the limiting beliefs of worry and doubt about what may go wrong.

Encourage the Pull to Growth - Infinite intelligence has implanted and embedded within each of us a pull to growth. If we are not expanding, we are contracting. A steady state is just a misnomer for a gradual decline. We are given the daily responsibility to serve one or more of the four dimensions in our full spectrum life. We choose how to apply the concepts freely to relationships, health and wellness, and time and money freedom as well as the business and philanthropy dimension.

Expand your day-to-day routine - for better or worse, we have results. To honor the pull to growth we need to alter our day-to-day routine to find the capacity for growth. This can take a variety of forms. For example, as a senior leader, I often allowed my client and colleagues to fill my 8 AM- 5 PM calendar with meetings. Most were necessary, appropriate, and even effective given the nature and scale of the work I was leading. However, that often meant that I also had a full schedule of work in the evening that was spent reviewing the work produced by my teams and fulfill other firm responsibilities meaning 80-hour work weeks were not uncommon. Now that I am self-employed, I have the opportunity to redefine my work calendar. Other challenges arise, how to complete all of the competing important categories of work; direct revenue generation, required operations, and indirect revenue generation activities. I notice that after years of practice prioritization is not an issue as much as capacity. I need to ask myself daily, what can I stop doing and delegate to someone else? What can be deferred to a future date and what must be done today in order to take on any new projects that will advance my business?

Return to Resiliency

Other habits we adopt as we age, whether through nurture, trauma, education, or experience have adverse impacts on our spine. We stiffen our spine to project strength or determination, and we do not move to another position frequently enough. We allow stress and worry to impact our physical health and our flexibility is contracted. We become inflamed both emotionally through unresolved anger, disappointment, failure, or perfectionism and that translates to real-life symptoms such as arthritis and other autoimmune diseases along with heart and other stress related illnesses. Illness is a flag that understanding how to adapt and retain our resilience and reach as leaders is essential in maintaining a healthy spine and our core values.

As we read through each of the steps in the innovation launch and value creation view of an expanded business vision, we will likely have identified points where resiliency will be required. We do not control the outcome, but we do control our attitude and the actions we take. We can remain contracted or we can leverage our resiliency, behave as innovation business leaders, and infuse our business with resiliency. The stories below serve as examples of resiliency and how we can apply these to our unique circumstances and situations.

Extend Our Time – Working with public sectors and nonprofit organizations often was a challenge. They tended to set overly ambitious time schedules to reduce the cost of the services they needed to hire. Their documentation requirements were also extensive. The key to success was counterintuitive, using the smallest most agile team. When one area of the client organization fell behind, the project manager could redirect the work and team to another aspect of the project to stall, without having to constantly renegotiate contract extensions. We earned a reputation for fairness in bidding that led to follow-up contracts because the client felt heard in their need to delay, without contention over the circumstances of the delay or situation for the vendor in not completing the contract before the budget ran out.

Expand Our Idea – while in consulting, a client was implementing a new technology designed to move their organization from paper to system- based operations. The overarching idea was to be able to offer new revenue generating services that would preserve jobs for 50% of their workforce, who were subject to budgetary-driven layoffs. Given the magnitude of the change and the fact that 94% of their workforce was unionized, there was anxiety and resistance to changing job design and roles. To minimize the impacts and increase understanding and awareness, it was critical to involve all of the business leaders from each area of the organization in deciding how work would be done, who would be doing the work, and communicating what training they would get. Each department was our customer, and we involved each area not only in the design but in the testing and rollout of the technology over the course of the year-long project. We worked with the HR executive to provide the communications required to change job roles, training, and the implications of why this project was important to the organization.

Despite following all of the best practices, union members decided to strike. The 6 % of the leadership who were not union members had the opportunity at times to drop the project, yet they stayed for the course because the alternative of losing 300 jobs was not tolerable. They believed that managing through a strike was preferable to losing 50% of their workforce. In the end, by ignoring the protests, continuing the project, and delivering clear consistent communications and increased engagement and training, the new system was implemented. The new business ventures they envisioned were launched and the jobs were saved.

Expand Our Product or Service - When we started the project to stand up a health insurance exchange for a state agency, we focused on agency workers and consumers and designed a software with two portals. The worker portal was focused on efficient data entry while a consumer was on the phone to limit the time it took to complete an application. As the agency grew from 7 to 57 employees and the federal interpretations of business rules emerged, it became clear that another portal was needed for choosing which agencies to use. Insurance brokers, navigators, and assisters had a vastly different way of working with their customers and a vastly different level of computer literacy. We developed a third portal for those users. It was a hybrid of the single question consumer portal and the busy data entry centric screen of the worker portal. In this case it was better to modify the software system design than to attempt to train users and extend the rental of training facilities around the state to reach out to all users for longer periods of time.

Forward Memory

Developing and holding a full spectrum vision for our life is the key to aligning our spine, or core values in our expanded life. We typically think of memory as only a backwards mental faculty. We memorize facts, details, and names. Yet, there is an even more powerful aspect of memory, it is forward memory. When we were newborns, we needed hourly or frequent nurturing to grow. If we are a parent of a newborn, it would be ridiculous not to feed and change the newborn every hour or two. Our new vision requires that same level of nurture.

Memorize every aspect of this new life, the pictures that come, the feelings we have, the knowing that we did this, and what it meant to us, our family, and our friends to have accomplished this. Carefully note the file path to this memory in our memory banks.

Now that the memory is stored, it can be called upon by clicking on that neuronal pathway. Each time you access that memory, it hardwires your vision and places it front and center in your brain. You now have the ability to see the vision as complete. Create a memory reel of what it felt like to attain each interim milestone. Those are your milestone images to be filed away in the same area of your brain.

Athletes routinely employ this approach. For example, we hear golfers speak about how they visualize the shot. The golfer first judges the distance from the fairway onto the green, then add details like the shape of the shot out to the right to launch the ball out over a tree and land left of a greenside bunker and roll down towards the pin. To apply this to your business, you need the same level of detail and clarity. To launch a product for a child's outdoor toy, you may choose a last day of school launch if the weather plays a role when you use the toy. One milestone image is when we picture how the child will use the toy and incorporate that into our product specifications. Another may be picturing our target customer, if the price point is high enough that the child can't purchase it for themselves with their own money from chores, gifts, etc. then your marketing team focuses on how to pitch the toy to their parent or other relative to buy the toy for them. Now that we have our product and marketing images, maybe we need to develop a picture of the ideal investor to fund building the new product. Create that image in our mind, is the toy an improvement on an existing genre of toys or something completely new? Bankers may be the answer for a traditional toy that innovates joy, durability, or some other factor of a similar toy. Whereas, if it is new and outlandish, we may look at the other types of investors angel and venture capital depending on scale of the manufacturing process adjustments.

Resiliency is important as we as entrepreneurs and small business owners encounter on a regular basis. Resiliency is honoring the validity of our vision and using the mental faculty of will command ourselves to call upon something deep inside of us to try again.

Using Growth Model Principles

As business leaders, we want to grow and expand. In the growth model below, let us get a visual picture for how the model works.

Boredom Zone - To the bottom left we see the boredom zone; these are tasks that need to be done, yet do not provide the business owner with the intrinsic satisfaction that comes from owning a business. When we spend every day executing this class of tasks, we set up a pattern of repetition. We think the same thoughts every day, we execute the same routine. To grow we must break patterns like this, and we do that by looking at our organization and team. When we identify who has the capability and passion for these tasks, not only do they complete them accurately and effectively, but when they have a passion for the work, their ideas will serve to propel those aspects of the business forward more quickly and iteratively than we can by completing the work as we would a check list of actions to be completed before we can take on the tasks that we love to do.

Growth Zone – this is our target zone as business leaders. When we align our strategic plan to the company vision and mission, we have a starting point. Like a journey across the country, we begin with the end in mind and set the interim milestones and supporting actions that propel us forward. By breaking down even exponential growth vision into defined segments we set up the conditions for success and we can continue to define new opportunities to expand because we have set in place the vibrational energy that continues to iteratively grow and expand.

Comfort Zone – this is our yellow flag zone. We know that life is either growing or contracting. Steady state is a myth. Other businesses in our industry and market will continue to grow as well. When we do not identify the strategy and aligned plans that propel us forward, we immediately move into contraction. We shift our energy to the classic "prevent defense" from football and begin to play small. We take the safe route, we do not strive to be more, do more, and give more to our customers. A new mindset for decision-making comes into play. We play not to fumble, not to get an interception, and we overlook the open receiver in the end zone and throw a quick out to the tight end. This makes us predictable and increases the likelihood that other businesses will identify our new more defensive and conservative strategy and end up turning the tables for the victory.

Overwhelm Zone - is when we have taken on too much. There are a few drivers, such as shooting for the stars without defining what the milestones are. Without those guideposts, we may veer off course ever so slightly in the comfort zone and not notice the yellow flags because we have not defined the targets in a way that allows u to understand that we are off the mark. In golf, we can line up a shot and be off at impact by as little as a 1/16 of an inch and the result can be a badly missed shot. This sets up a series of recovery actions to get us back on track. Another way to get into the overwhelm zone is to ignore the tasks in the boredom zone, rather than assigning them to someone who will ensure they get done. Not entering daily transactions on a single day is not make or break, but if we continue to prioritize other tasks over those on a regular basis, we can fall one or more months behind. We lose track of the documentation or details and cannot take advantage of all of the knowledge we would have had, if done in the moment. We may also have an issue with setting boundaries. We want to please our team, our customers, vendors, etc. and lose sight of our capacity. There may be nothing inherently inappropriate in any single task, contract, or transaction yet if we lose sight of the valid exceptions and repeat these decisions, we set up the conditions for overwhelm. This is an issue that was not caught in the comfort zone but has not yet reached critical state.

Expand and breakthrough limiting beliefs

John W. Gardner was the Secretary of Health, Education, and Welfare under President Lyndon Johnson and a recipient of the 1964 Presidential Medal of Freedom. In this passage, he describes the importance of tough-minded optimism:

"Optimism is unfashionable today, particularly among intellectuals. Everyone makes fun of it. Someone said, "Pessimists got that way by financing optimists." But I am not pessimistic, and I advise you not to be...a tough-minded optimism is best. The future is not shaped by people who do not really believe in the future. People of vitality have always been prepared to bet their futures, even their lives, on ventures of unknown outcome. If they had all looked before they leaped, we would still be crouched in caves sketching animal pictures on the wall. But I did say tough-minded optimism. High hopes that are dashed by the first failure are precisely what we do not need. We have to believe in ourselves, but we must not suppose that the path will be easy, it is tough. Life is painful, and rain falls on the just, and Mr. Churchill was not being a pessimist when he said, "I have nothing to offer, but blood, toil, tears and sweat." He had a great deal more to offer, but as a good leader he was saying it wasn't going to be easy, and he was also saying something that all great leaders say constantly — that failure is simply a reason to strengthen resolve."

Our mental faculty of will is the ability to make ourselves to do the actions we do not like or prefer in service of the greater goal. Often, we misconstrue will as willpower. Willpower is the opposite of will, it is a subjugation of our will. Willpower can only be accomplished in small bursts and is not sustainable. We say we are exercising willpower when we deny ourselves a piece of birthday cake when we want it. However, the opposite is true; we want the piece of birthday cake and we are suppressing our will by denying our desire for it. We can do without cake, bread, and potatoes for a week to look good for an important event, but really, a life without ever celebrating your birthday by eating cake, hardly not.

Our mental faculty of will allows us to focus. We choose the area of focus. It may be on the burning desire to solve your customers' problems or to set a larger goal of making social change and impact through your work. Then on a day-to-day basis I am choosing to make phone calls and learn accounting and business principles in service of achieving these larger goals. If you find that you have difficulties in learning the required skills, then an action you can take is to decide whether it's better to take a class or try outsourcing the task to a vendor who already knows it works better for you. Making the right decisions propel your business to overcome the statistical odds.

Each of the examples in each zone we just reviewed depend on the quality of the actions we take. The Law of Attraction notes that the speed of results is proportionate to the amount of the action we take. If we generate a fleeting thought or idea, it has some mass. Using balls as an example, it may be the mass of a whiffle ball. If we continue to work with that fleeting thought to build it into a concept, that weight may be similar to a tennis ball. When we fill in the actions and add emotion, we see that the mass increases to that of a baseball. When we add emotion, purpose, repetition, and intention we then have the mass of a softball.

A limiting belief can cause us to take less effective, safer actions, which are most likely to be less effective in achieving the vision. They also can move us into indecision. While we know that the lack of a decision is actually a decision, a delayed decision can miss the opportunity and render the decision a moot point. Inaction can often the root cause of failure, we put off doing what we do not know how to do and focus on answering emails or something we know. We do not like to do one aspect of our business, so it always ends up at the bottom of our to do list. Let us review a few common limiting beliefs and their impact on our results.

Circumstances – how many times in life are all of the conditions perfect? The answer is almost never. We as leaders make tough decisions with incomplete information, lack of an ideal business model, and lack of the perfect team or defined our perfect customer. When we are a new company we don't have a long history to promote in our marketing, we don't have all of the pieces defined, yet when we breakthrough the idea that everything must be perfect, before we take any action, we breakthrough that limiting belief. We take the action or actions need to fill in the gaps, instead of using that as an excuse to avoid risk and action.

Confidence – we may have had a failure either in our past or recently that makes us gun shy of repeating that experience. Maybe we are expanding into an area that requires expanded capability and we lack confidence in our ability to deliver on our promises and keep our word. To breakthrough in this area requires a different set of actions. It requires introspection to see what we can do to build our confidence. The correct actions are to set up the right qualitative and quantitative measures to measure progress. This gives you data to match your intuition and increase your confidence.

Competition – looking at what our competition does rather than adhering to your vision is a limiting belief. It sets up the scenario when you are giving the competition too much space in your head. If we do not have competition, we do not have a business. If no one else is doing it, it is likely because there is no market for your product or service. Flipping the perspective to genuinely believe that competition is a good thing and understanding what you do better, either as a business leader or as a business, is a great action to take to breakthrough.

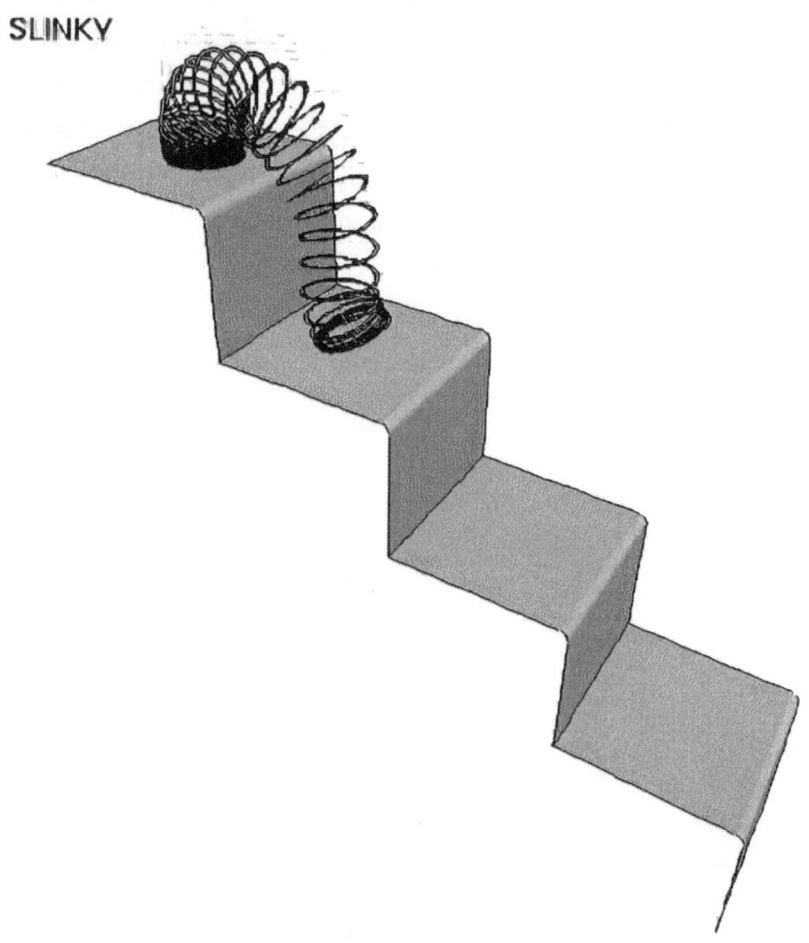

CHAPTER FIVE
ENERGIZE

Energy inspires movement and action

One of the properties that has sustained the Slinky® over time is its ability to move. It captures our imagination when it goes down stairs or hangs suspended in mid air. Both of those properties were directly opposite of what the designer was trying to achieve in his work project. Yet, he was so captivated by these properties, it inspired him to leave that position and start his own firm. What is it about that mindset that you have that inspires and drives you to new expressions of creativity and leads you to take actions that lead to a level of success that others around you do not experience?

Prime for Growth Not Comfort

The comfort zone is a dangerous place. Known is good, unknown is somewhere on a scale from exciting to paralyzing with fear for the most vulnerable. I chose the word exciting intentionally as that word connotes an element of fear or anxiety about the unknown, even if we are also happy. Think back to the first time we stepped up to home plate as a batter in a softball or baseball game. We were excited. Would we strike out? Would we hit a home run? Would the crowd cheer or would they boo? It is the same when we step out in any new venture, speaking on stage, singing in public, speaking in a large meeting on an important topic. It can magnify our doubts when it comes to decisions like is my mission _____ (fill in the blank with big enough, good enough) to ask for _____(sponsors, donors, money, volunteers, etc.).

The comfort zone in our mindset minimizes risk. The story we tell ourselves is that we are good now and growth carries the implied risk of failure. How is it that we let a past failure linger in our minds far longer and give it far more weight than a past success? My mentor, Mary Morrissey, tells a short tale relating to this. When we were babies, we crawled then we pulled ourselves up and stood, then we tried to walk. We took a step, we fell, we got up, we took a step, maybe two, and fell again. And not once, not ever did it cross our minds over the days, weeks, or however long it took to master walking, no matter how many times we fell as we moved from carpet to wood floors or wood to tile or some other surface. As we tried to go faster, slow down, move up an uneven surface, or whatever circumstance or situation we encountered did we ever just sit down and say to ourselves "Well, I guess I'm just not meant to be a walker". When did that focus on failure or setbacks creep in? When did we allow it to take hold?

The cost of the comfort zone is the opportunity cost. It is hard to calculate in quantifiable dollars and cents, but we know it is real and we can measure it. It is in the number of unserved clients. It is the number of unopened locations for our business. It is the number of callers who sat on hold and could not get through to donate. It is the unsold books because our book is sitting half-written on our laptop or rolling around in our head. It is the aches and pains we experience each morning as symptoms of an unlived life of purpose and clarity. It is the number of hours we lay awake at night wishing, hoping, and longing with the discontent of not making a larger impact with the work we are doing today, because we are diluting each action by multi-tasking in the hopes of completing 30 tasks that take two hours each in a 24-hour day. When we look at the comfort zone in this way, we immediately recognize the risks of living a good life in the known. The growth zone is, by definition, anywhere but our comfort zone. Let us look at some strategies for energizing ourselves to become better leaders and how to keep ourselves, our team, and our business energized in an iterative pattern.

Vitality Equals Relevance

As leaders we can adopt several strategies for promoting health and wellness. First, we focus on our own health and wellness. To me it is creating a vision for what health and wellness is to you. For me, I value restful sleep that provides the stamina and energy to wake up refreshed. To get a good night's sleep, I review my day hour-by-hour. If there was something that went great, I acknowledge my gratitude for that outcome. If something did not go well or remains unresolved, I set my intention to put that in the past and think about opportunities for how to create a different experience tomorrow. I rehearse the new ways of thinking about that situation, rather than reviewing what did not work.

Finally, I set my intention for the next day. This allows my subconscious to have free reign overnight to prime me for the right mindset and actions that are required. Other ways I support my health are by eating tasty, healthy fresh food, incorporating movement throughout the day versus being chained to an office desk chair and laptop, being in nature for some period of time every day, and being rigorous with my mindset when it drifts into unfocused, negative, or constrained thoughts. Develop a mental trigger that causes you to review your mindset. Is it every time you see a keyboard, before you tap out a text, email, or other communication? Another option for a mental trigger is selecting a handle as a visual cue. For example, every time you see a handle, you create a visual cue to trigger your mind to know that you have a handle on your mindset.

It is about designing a ritual that replenishes my soul, body, and mind. I am not recommending that this is the specific routine for everyone, some may have specific athletic goals that enter into the equation, others are in recovery from an illness, trauma, or accident that demands extra focus to define what the new normal will be for their situation.

When we have our health and wellness routine and vision in place, we can then be a model for our team members to adopt a strategy and plan for achieving their vision. They see how we incorporate the activities that are directly related into our calendar and they can see the results when we always show up, how we show up committed and focused, and how we value adhering to a work calendar that respects our common need to place importance on the other three dimensions of our full-spectrum life.

We can also set the tone in the culture of the team we create. We set flexibility and predictability into our work routine as well. Emails and phone calls end at the end of the workday with defined, infrequent, and well-communicated exceptions. We celebrate successes and develop the training, career path, and succession plans that create an environment where traditional salary and benefits are not the decision criteria for your applicants. They can become a part of the team that drives results and success.

Energize by Sourcing the Right Talent

Attracting, recruiting, and sourcing the right talent is often an overlooked function of the entrepreneur or business leader. We craft a website and sales materials that focus on attracting the right target customer. This is essential to drive revenue, yet, we spend little time each workday with an individual customer, unless we are a coach, consultant, teacher, or other similar profession. Even if we choose to outsource the function to a recruiting agency or automate the screening of applicants, we would do well to invest in creating an avatar employee profile similar to our avatar client profile for each position.

Instead of looking around us to identify who they are, identifying the skills and capabilities are required are easier to describe in this exercise. We also have access to a number of template job description sources online. Yet, there is more to it in a small company. There is the impact of personality on the culture of a small venture. Cultural fit is important and difficult to measure. Some ideas to think about for measures are accountability, communication styles, taking a job to completion, pitching in outside of a defined set of job responsibilities. While these are sometimes more abstractly defined concepts, they are important to think through as you define the job role and your ideal candidate. When we are trying to hire people with an entrepreneurial attitude, part of this will be about inherent personalities: who the person is. Identifying what qualities, the person embodies is a part of your description. Curiosity, persistence, and humor are examples of these types of qualities that have a large impact on small organizations by size.

Here is some non-threatening, innovate questions you may consider when interviewing your shortlist of candidates. As a kid, did that person mow lawns or babysit constantly? Are they always growing and building things? This might be a for-profit business, but it might also be community-building, changing their local community for the better. These are activities that you can ask a candidate about as you get to know them, to see if they bring a problem-solving attitude to all aspects of their life.

Creativity and growth mindset techniques can be taught and therefore learned. By learning and applying creative thinking processes, we can teach creativity. Take this one step further, and we realize that we can teach our employees to think and work like entrepreneurs. This is crucial, because we are not going to replace our entire workforce if we are an established business. We would not want to even if we could. What we can do is identify the people who are already thinking entrepreneurially and design the mentor or training programs to help teach others how to be more entrepreneurial in their approach.

CEO as a Player - In the early days of a startup company, we might have 3 to 10 employees. During that time period, everyone, including the CEO, is responsible for many different tasks. At this stage, in addition to helping manage the team, the CEO is spending a significant percentage of their time doing more low-level tasks such as finding a new office, selling product to customers, and paying the bills.

CEO as a Player-Coach - As a company makes progress and the team grows, the CEO sheds many of his/her low-level tasks and spends a higher percentage of his/her time managing the team. The company is starting to put processes in place and build out more traditional departments like sales, product development, customer success, finance, marketing, etc. Some departments have VPs running them, others do not. The CEO still needs to play multiple roles, but only in a utility role. More of the CEO's time is spent creating the game plan, recruiting the talent, and coaching the players.

CEO as a Coach - When a company reaches the stage where it moves to a more structured organization with lots of processes in place, the CEO has limited time to work on specific projects. No longer does the CEO perform multiple roles. Their role is 100% focused on creating the game plan, recruiting the talent, and coaching the players.

Brainstorming as a Core Competency of Wealth

When circumstances or situations arise that challenge the foundation of our business, brainstorming is an effective approach. Yet it only works when we are open to new ideas, rather than relying on our established internal patterns. The question becomes - How do we break out of the mental patterns and operate in neutral mode, even when our emotions and experience are screaming in our head that this is bad?

For me, one thing that has worked consistently, is to find a period in time when I have memories of being safe, secure, and joyful. That time is about age six for me. I enjoyed having a structure for my curious nature, where the questions, why, how, etc. were encouraged. A full day school instead of half day was an improvement for me.

My favorite way to create the luxury of responding, versus reacting, is to ask myself how my six-year-old self would like to see the situation and options play out. When decision time can be scheduled for the next day, I amplify the benefits and ask myself this question before I go to sleep and let me dreams guide me. If same day decision making is desired, then I do the exercise while meditating or being still.

Why does this work for me? As a six-year-old, I do not have the reasoning to shut down the dreams when I ask myself - what I would love to make happen? At that age, I still believed in all possibilities. This act opens my perspective and takes the blinders off.

Now that I have the possibilities, the important thing is to document every single idea, without allowing any editing by your adult persona. Just let the ideas flow for a minimum of 20 minutes, or whenever after that point the ideas stop flowing. If after five minutes the ideas pause, just continue to be still. This patience is required to get beyond the practical, relatively obvious ideas and into a more profound connection.

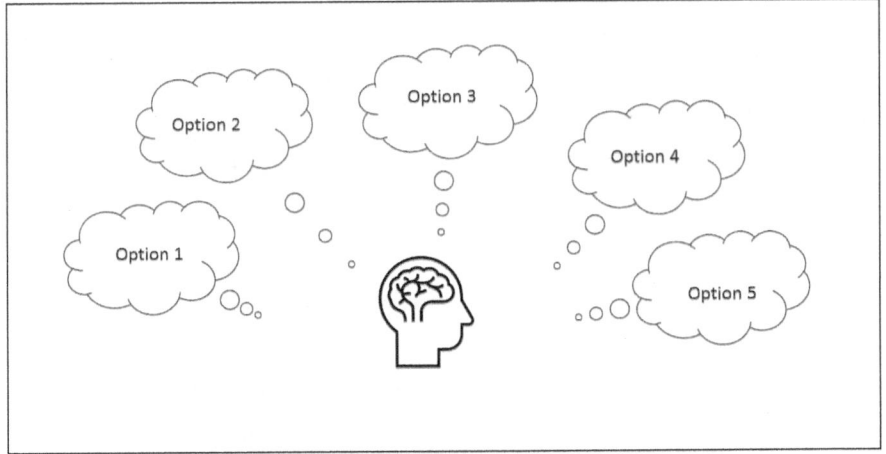

Without attaching any emotion to any of the ideas, take a look, while you are in that deeper level of consciousness to see which of these options, at first glance, seems to satisfy the disconnect, longing, or other situation you are addressing. Rank them by this perspective. Let us say the ideas above resonate for you.

The next action is to gently hold each of these actions in your mind concurrently. See if there is any overlap, intersection, or potential conflict between them. Picture a standard Venn diagram. In this way, you will be able to create a visual overlay of the ideas. Where the circles intersect is where the sweet spot is. How does that align with your adult vision for where you need to lead your organization? Does it get you to your end goal or vision? Does it get you to a milestone along the way? Or does it raise a new perspective to consider that may alter the direction you were headed? What are the risks and issues that arise when identifying potential concerns? What activities have the potential, through synergies, to exponentially elevate your actions and effectiveness? What can we see to avoid redundancy and overlap?

The goal is to quickly notice when we make a shift from growth to constraint when we move into our comfort zone. When we notice, then we can put in place the appropriate actions that slide us back into an expanded growth zone. After noticing, then the key is to refocus our attention back to our value chain. Once we are focused on our values, we can see what is out of alignment. That is the weakest link in the chain today. Then we can source the ideas and actions that can propel us forward in that area. If a risk is noted, document it so it does not get filed away in the far reaches of our mind. If we file it away, it just sits in the back of our mind collecting fear, doubt, and worry momentum. Instead, I invite us to acknowledge it and set a time on our calendar to address the risk(s) that we have noted in our log. This way, we will keep the ideas and actions coming with the knowledge that we have also scheduled a meeting to deal with the risks. This approach is not about playing ostrich and denying circumstances and situations, it is about proactively overcoming them.

At the end of 30-60 minutes we now have a comprehensive list of potential actions. The key to this exercise, as with any good brainstorming exercise, is to not edit. If this is a team exercise, then the unedited unfiltered approach is still key. This includes no rolling eyes or other judgmental body language that shuts down input.

If this exercise is done on our own, write everything down that comes to mind, even if it seems random. At first, we will get the analytic side of our brain coming out. If we stick with it, even if there are pauses in the stream or flow of ideas, resist the temptation to be "productive" and move onto something else. As I have worked with this over time, I noticed that the accountant and engineering process-oriented side of my brain let go after a while and the people, creative side of my brain would then have space to speak up. That side of my personality whispers so I try to create the conditions that allow me to be quiet long enough to really pick up on what it is sending me.

If this does not work in the middle of the workday, look at other options. During a commute I turn on calming music and set an expectation that I will be moving slowly, and I enjoy the peace between work and home. Now that I have created this space, instead of taking phone calls, I get ideas, like how one piece of the puzzle connects to another in my mind. It just happens gracefully and easily, when I allow that freedom in my calendar and in my mind. For others it maybe early in the morning or late at night when the rest of the house is asleep. The goal is to write everything down without editing.

I find that the next step works best for me after a break. If I let the list sit, move on with other known activities that are already identified as moving the business and mission forward, and clear my mind of any preconceived resonance, priorities are identified in a new, fresh order. When we are ready, pick the list back up, review it, and just check any of the ideas that feel expansive today. These are actions that feel as though they would propel our business and/or mission forward to growth. These are not just the actions that would be fun, but actions that bring energy of growth, not contraction.

While we are our own best judge of what visions, milestones, and actions energize us and are needle movers that create the conditions for success, letting our team, trusted advisors, and customers in and being receptive to their ideas not only creates values when their idea drives successful outcomes, but it also demonstrates your respect for their capabilities and ideas and builds a long-term relationship.

Priming Our Attitude to Energize Our Actions

We can use several techniques to prime our attitude for success. We can use inspirational quotes, affirmations, etc. to prime our minds each morning and on stressful days throughout the day to stay on course and bring a spirit of high energetic vibration to the day. We can also incorporate setting intentions, reducing stress through exercise, meditation, and other actions to mentally prepare for the day ahead.

There is a lot of press about the overnight successes, but the reality is that being an entrepreneur and business leader is about the hard, often lonely, work in between the few moments of clarity and celebration. Being able to thrive in those less-than-newsworthy periods in between the moments of celebration is what makes a successful entrepreneur. It is about continuous disciplined execution—and that is not easy. Raising our energetic state is a core capability for us to adopt. Each of the activities noted can be done in a process for really stressful moments or times, or in short bursts throughout the day as needed. I also recommend incorporating many of these into your daily routine to even out your energetic state and maintain the vibrations needed to reach your vision.

Breathe - there is a well-known process of rectangular breathing that provides calmness and steadiness in times of stress. Breathe deeply in through your nose. This signals to your body that there is no threat or danger. Exhales through your mouth to fully release the pent-up stress. As you repeat this several times, you will feel yourself calming down. If you are in the throes of self-sabotage, on the inhales begin to say to yourself your affirmation statement that applies to the circumstance or situation. It can be something as simple as, "This is what it looks like when it is all coming together". Another option is "I am bringing my very best to _____ and my best is enough" . This is a great technique before a planned interaction that has the potential to generate conflict.

Meditate - During those low points, the first thing to hit us is generally the feeling of complete defeat or anxiety. Often, we cannot even articulate what it is that is causing it, but it does not actually matter. The feeling is there and that is the challenge. When this happens, we are in a state of amygdala-hijack and we are in full primal flight-or-fight mode, which renders us pretty useless at making good decisions and thinking sensibly. If we give in, we invite lower vibrations to take hold and hijack our day.

So, I choose to find a quit place to meditate. By meditating, even for five minutes, I allow my brain the chance to shift its energy away from the amygdala (fight-or-flight), toward the pre-frontal cortex (awareness, concentration, and clear decision making). Simply put, if I give myself the time to meditate, I move out of panic and into calm. There are quite a few apps to guide meditation (Mind Movies, Calm, and Dr. Joe Dispenza to name a few), but there are plenty of ways to meditate without any tools.

Movement – Sometimes we need something other than stillness to break the mood. Take a break and move, put on your favorite upbeat dance song, and move, take a quick run, swim, or workout to rid your body of the hormone burst you just experienced in fight-or-flight mode.

Improve my environment - turn our attention to our immediate physical environment. Is my workspace filling up with stacks of papers, Post-It note reminders that did not make into my calendar or other triggers for a cluttered mind as a result of a cluttered workspace? We can take a few minutes to properly tidy and clean our workspace. Here is why.

We think that our attention and thinking causes our feelings. Those feelings control our actions and, we do have the ability to change our environment and improve our attention and thinking to change our feelings. The underlying cause of your stress maybe that you are missing something. By cleaning up your workspace, adding any Post-It notes to your overall plan, calendar, etc. puts those actions back in their place. You free up brain cycles that are trying to remember the time for an important call by documenting it on your calendar. This restores energetically a sense of order and control in your mind.

Reflect and be grateful - Now that we are sitting at an organized workspace and feeling good about our physical surroundings, we can stop to appreciate that we have taken difficult and deliberate action to improve our state of being— this is more than most are prepared to do. Now we can reflect on some of the positive things that we have achieved and experienced in our lives. By this stage, our brain is truly beginning to shift. The amygdala is losing its control to my good friend the pre-frontal cortex. Here I often remind myself, "What got me here won't get me there", which always helps me to affect more change.

Set my intentions for the day - By this stage we are thinking more clearly. The world, while not perfect, does not seem to be burning down around us. We turn to our ever-loyal whiteboard and write down our intentions for the day.

This will stay on our whiteboard (or whichever medium makes sense) throughout the day allowing us to focus on activities that are needle movers designed to help us progress and move forward. At the end of the day, we complete a quick reflection to see how we did on each item. We also reflect on which tasks increased my energy and which drained my energy. Setting intentions and reflecting is a habit that can become part of our daily life and its effects have been astounding.

Make things smaller - Use a tool like a daily planner, calendar,

Trello, or other app to manage our personal tasks, goals, habits, etc. The idea here is to make tasks extremely granular and therefore manageable. I find that many people have a challenge in taking a concept like making a customer happy and putting that into tasks that fit onto a calendar. It is the same with any relationship. We schedule dates, sports, dinners, play and activities with ease and fill our calendars up. But does that make our marriage better, our kids happy or our relationships stronger?

Sometimes it does, they key to the task is discovering the underlying value behind the activity. I like going out to eat with my husband. Why? It has nothing to do with the food, it is because we do not take our phones or our television with us. We sit across the table and for the time we are there, we talk to one another. If we went to a sports bar or brought our phones, i would rather be at home. It is about the connection, so when we break down the task to its smaller unit it must be about the point of the task, connection, and the value we are trying to accomplish.

Now take a fresh look at what you have scheduled, does the set of activities align to getting you to your vision? Are you focusing on what you value? If so, we are generally in a better mindset we are confident that the activities on our calendar take our values and split them into actionable tasks. Now we have a basis to measure progress. This builds confidence, and clarity because we now understand that what we are doing aligns to our values.

If not, we may notice that the list is excessively long, or that we have added things to the list that are future tasks. Maybe we want a new floor layout for the retail business to create social distancing and we are overwhelmed. The way that we can go about this is to make a list of the all the things that need to get done in order to move the needle on the areas that got me into this negative headspace in the first place. Then we divide them into two groups: Things we can change. Things we cannot change. This next part is crucial: The things that we cannot change, we delete and give them up to the universe. If we cannot affect change on an issue, it is nothing short of insane to worry about it.

We cannot change government regulations, the lack of a vaccination for COVID, etc. so we need to let go of the resistance. The list should contain things like, reviewing sales figures and determining what items have not been selling well and may be candidates for discounts and future discontinuation. Determine the items to feature to increase sales, determine items that naturally fit together in your customers minds' to increase sales and match the overhead directions to the new layout.

Now that we have released ourselves from the things we cannot change, we focus on the things that are within our locus of control and we break these tasks down to the smallest tasks that we can. We proceed with the goal of being able to put the tasks on our calendar in a manner that gets things done.

Each time that we complete even the smallest task, we get a little hit of dopamine and a sense of improvement which then incentivizes us to get the next one done. So, the upward spiral of positive action and feeling begins. I often select the activities I am most resistant to doing first, while my motivation is back in alignment. This reinforces my progress rather than having a task I do not want to do looming over my head.

This entire process can take as little as an hour and the effects for me, every time, are transformational. The hardest part by far is getting started. If we can stop what we are doing (freaking out) and give yourself the gift of focused, mindful self-observation and disciplined action, the rest follows naturally. It is pretty incredible how things begin to miraculously fall into place after that. Trust the process.

Energize by taking time away - We contribute in a variety of ways to the success of our business and the social impact we desire, but to live a full spectrum life with healthy self, relationships, and time and money freedom, stepping away for planned time off is vital to success in each dimension. Honoring your vision for time and money freedom enables you to put in place the structures and culture that allow you as a leader to step away and have the business continue and thrive.

Taking time away means just that. It does not mean working a full work week remotely, answering emails, texts, participating on conference calls and other temptations to re-engage. Boundaries are great for weekends and other holidays and days off. My recommendation, which is backed up by studies, shows that two weeks together is an ideal scenario. The first two or three days is essentially withdrawal from the business. The next eight days or so are beginning to create the separation that provides inspiration and relaxation. The final three days we start to mentally re-engage unless we are disciplined in focusing on our time away.

The benefits extend to your external inbound information when you have a true delegate in place. When we as leaders are away for a short period of time, many employees, vendors, and customers will wait for your return and build some resistance to having to wait. Yet if you are gone for two weeks, they are much more likely to work with your delegate. This means that business continues on the standard rhythm and you are not typically inundated by pent-up demand upon your return.

Flipping our perspective

In each aspect or dimension of our lives, we experience the need for this capability. We control our perspective and when we can flip the perspective from limiting to expansive, we not only energize ourselves, but our team. In a limiting perspective we are focused on what is going wrong. In an expansive perspective we focus on what is going well. Either way, our perspective and our thinking control our feelings, our actions, and our results. If we focus on our problems, we get more problems. If we focus on what is going well, we get more success.

When I was listening to a conference call the other day, the premise was that nonprofits are experts in managing scarcity. In that sector the pervasive mindset is that there is always too much need and too little in the way of contribution to match the need. The fundamental acceptance of not having enough is a part of their system of belief. We can't have the financial system we want because we can't raise enough funds, we can't attract good talent, because smart people don't work for nonprofits, we have to accept manual processes because we have to intervene because we don't have enough money to pay the bills, etc. Many of us will resonate with that in our social business.

Let us challenge that premise. As social business leaders, we are responsible for reframing that perspective. We are called to be resilient and flexible and challenge that thinking by planting another visual image in the minds of our cause and in our customers. We are not called to ignore the challenges of raising donations or running a profitable business. We are called to see new opportunities in how we address the business challenges. We have access to everything we need, when we take the blinders off and break through old patterns of where our attention is directed and old thought patterns, we create different results.

Here is an example: Those of us who have businesses focused on disaster recovery know that Mother Nature has patterns when tornados, hurricanes, earthquakes, and forest fires are most likely to occur, yet lightening can and will strike anywhere. Identifying the risks, staging the supplies and services, and creating a flexible network that can go from zero to 100 miles an hour as the weather demands creates a unique business model and relies on establishing strong business partnerships not only for funding but for sourcing and distribution. There is not a reasonable city that would launch a new customer service application for their public safety department in the middle of a hurricane, or is there? I gave the go ahead to our project manager to go live with our call center application in the middle of hurricane Gustav in TX. The city was implementing the system because they did not have a good way to centrally coordinate the dispatch of emergency assistance across agencies. The police and fire departments each had their own dispatch systems, the water and sewer systems each had a different system, and consumers did not understand whether it was a water pipe or a sewer line that was the cause of a problem. Calls were routed between systems slowing response time. Facilities had another system. We worked with the city to implement a single system and to develop the correct call scripts to help the members of the community understand how to reach the right personnel and report an issue. The planned start date was a few weeks away, but with a hurricane moving in, and test results generally positive, we decided together that the new system could manage the demands of public safety and rescue calls better than what was in place today. We made a new decision as leaders; we stood together on a nontraditional path and made the right decision. Was it perfect? Not quite, but in the end, even with power loss and emergency generator back up running the system, all calls got answered and lives were saved.

Other aspects of social businesses focus on advancing healthcare. Scientific research is advancing in general; however, our life and family may be impacted by a disease that is not advancing as quickly as another and we are called to advance that mission and make a direct impact. Identifying the donors who resonate with our cause and have the resources is challenging. There are new modalities in functional medicine, naturopaths, food as medicine, and nutritional advice with conflicting studies. Quite often as a social business we need to uncover not only the veracity of the study but the agenda of the funding for the study. In this model our best entry point for impact may look tangled in our mind. The goal of using this approach is to be able to absorb and flex our mindset, plans, and approach without losing sight of our mission and creating a model in our mind that focuses on our outcome and allows for expansion and adjustment.

Other models of social businesses are rising where the business purpose is not social, yet the profits fund a social cause. One of the more well-known pioneers of this model is the Tom's shoe company. Based on the success of this and many other companies and a model of what is known as Corporate Social Responsibility that started decades ago and has become a recruiting hallmark for many companies and firm today, more and more of these corporate structures are being formed every day as new businesses launch.

The competition is great, the need is great, even in a reasonably strong economy, but not everyone benefits equally. Studies have been conducted to identify what separates those who thrive from those who falter. Those of us who have worked in consulting for years and/or who have attempted to make a large-scale change and encountered major resistance know the real answer – mindset. It is all about thinking in a certain way. We are certain of our vision, our plan, and the steps we are taking, yet not attached to any particular step or outcome and something even better still may be around the next corner.

Diversity, Equity, and Inclusion – we often limit our understanding of this important topic to a few dimensions. Race, gender, ethnicity, and the legal ramifications of compliance. I attended a symposium recently in Atlanta that was run by the Center for Healthcare Innovation (CHI). They shared the following set of definitions that I believe can be universally adopted for consistency in understanding.

Diversity - Diversity is the range of human differences, including but not limited to race, ethnicity, gender, gender identity, sexual orientation, age, social class, physical ability, or attributes, religious or ethical values system, national origin, and political beliefs.

Equity – the quality of being fair or just. In business fairness is not necessarily equal. You may need to invest more in outreach and communications to go beyond sameness and create a culture of welcoming to get to the same outcome in reaching a diverse set of clients or employees.

Inclusion - Inclusion is involvement and empowerment, where the inherent worth and dignity of all people are recognized. An inclusive organization promotes and sustains a sense of belonging; it values and practices respect for the talents, beliefs, backgrounds, and ways of living of its members.

THE SLINKY® EFFECT

This Photo by Unknown Author is licensed under CC BY-SA

Gender – there are multiple dimensions of gender that are being more widely recognized.

1. Gender Identity - Gender identity is the personal sense of one's own gender. If we are Cisgender, our personal sense and our biological gender are aligned. Transgender is when that is a mismatch. Non-binary is a spectrum of gender identities that are not exclusively masculine or feminine—identities that are outside the gender binary. Genderqueer is an earlier term with the same meaning.
2. Gender Expression - Gender expression is a person's behavior, mannerisms, interests, and appearance that are associated with gender in a particular cultural context, specifically with the categories of femininity or masculinity. This also includes gender roles. These categories rely on stereotypes about gender.
3. Biological Sex - In general terms, "sex" refers to the biological differences between males and females, such as the genitalia and genetic differences.

4. Sexual Orientation - a person's sexual identity in relation to the gender to which they are attracted; the fact of being heterosexual, homosexual, or bisexual.

From a business perspective, there are additional complexities to be considered when we desire to create a diverse, equitable, and inclusive culture. Standard forms typically only offer binary gender options for hiring, purchasing and in the case of healthcare, admission to the practice or hospital for care. From an external perspective, this is inherently unwelcoming, and they do not see themselves as your avatar client or employee. The transition process to align a person's gender identity and biological sex requires multiple years, including a year where the person lives as the other gender via their expression. During this time, there is often a mismatch between the person's legal name and their preferred name and identity. 11% have a correct ID, 49% have no ID in chosen name, and 67% are misaligned at some level (e.g. DL is correct and passport and other documents are not). In addition, 78% have requested HRT therapy, 49% are done with HRT, and 75% have had no physical transition or HRT. 10% of millennials report as non-binary.

During the transition, in addition to the challenges at screening and intake, most businesses have yet to take the challenges of restroom usage, violence, and lack of processes and other governance issues that make it difficult to focus on work and instead create internal stresses in dealing with a work environment that just doesn't understanding the needs and challenges of investing in creating an environment that is productive and welcoming.

As business leaders we have an opportunity to take our ideal of a diverse, equitable, and inclusive work environment and put actions into place that change the forms, policies, websites and lobby décor by educating our teams and demonstrating that this is more than hypothetical, it is real and tangible as part of how we design our business model and culture.

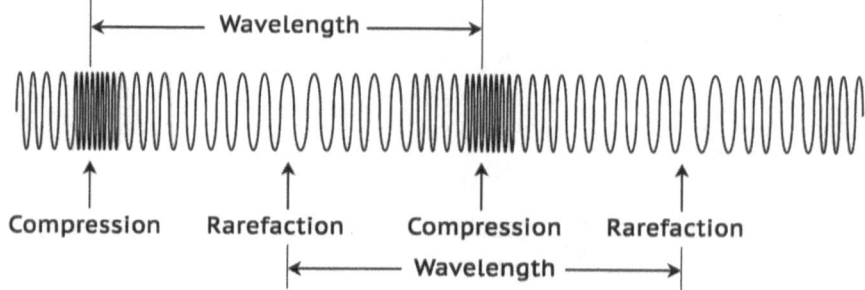

CHAPTER SIX
EMPOWER

Empower New Thinking

Scientists have been inspired by the engineering and math principles that underpin this toy and have taught classes and use the principles underscored in the lead in picture in their classrooms. How can we apply the metaphor of empowerment to business leadership?

Empower Through Understanding

Early in my career I was an accountant and began implementing Enterprise Resource Planning (ERP) software systems to provide better financial reporting and decision-making. At the time, in the mid 1990's, customers tended to run into large time budget overruns because they customized the "new" system to function in the same way as their old system because their executive leaders only had access to past performance data. Not surprisingly, when the project was over, their project satisfaction rating on a scale of 1-10 was typically around a 3. The chief complaint was that at the beginning of the project, when most key decisions were made, we did not know what we did not know. My company listened and as a result, I was part of a pioneer group for business transformation and organization change that worked with business leaders prior to the start of their project. We reversed the process and started by asking, "What is our vision for where our business will be in 5 years?" (yes, this was pre-internet boom and a realistic time frame then rather than the three-year timeframe of today.). Then we looked at their current processes and whether it worked for them or not. Then we looked at how well their organization structure would work to support their new vision (e.g. moving from national to global; brick and mortar to online.). Then we took the next step and helped them review all the ERP vendors (there were more players back then) and helped them determine an object scoring model that took internal politics out of the decision and based it on organization vision and their strategic direction. Then, when the team came in to work the project, the leaders were better prepared to make better decisions. Client satisfaction raised to an 8.

We all know people who live their lives like that. We see them occasionally, maybe at a store in town, a family holiday dinner, or a class reunion, and after about five minutes, we have caught up with them since there is really nothing to say, because they have lived unexpanded, contracted lives. They did not put their attention or control on any mission and their results are pretty much the same. Now, let us look an example of controlled action.

Solving our clients' business needs

A client I worked with had a strategic vision for business transformation that was quite complex. They were embarking on adding a new software that would track all of their assets and all of the tools, equipment, and labor that would maintain and add assets over time. We created an overall project plan that identified all of the tasks involved in designing the software configuration, redesigning the business processes around the new software and a comprehensive organization change and learning program that would empower the users to understand not only the new software, but how it could advance their business in alignment with the strategic vision. The project took 15 months to install, train, and empower their organization at all levels to change the way work orders were assigned, assets capitalized, and improve the response time to their customers' service calls.

There are keys in the above examples that set-in motion the conditions for empowerment. Defining a robust vision is key and the focus of this chapter, but that would not make for a whole book. The other aspects of being empowered is our understanding of how our personal life and business life are interwoven by capacity into a single vision. Another key aspect is how a clear vision empowers true critical thinking versus default thought patterns of our business leadership. New software is a tool to empowerment, but we need to change our thinking and learn to grow to use it to the maximum operational effectiveness as we saw in the example. Both comparisons and reality checks are important components of the empowerment, harmonizing the vision across all lines of the business. In the example Human Resources, Supply Chain, Work Management, and IT all needed to understand in crisp detail what the vision was so they could make the appropriate decisions for how the business rules would be configured in the software and documented for changes to policies, procedures, and learning materials. If we fall into the trap of looking only at what will optimize our particular area of the business, we compromise the success of the overall strategic business vision. To create our own empowerment to rise above the concerns of our staff, budget, and timeline, we change our perspective.

Current Perspective	New Perspective
• See what I want in the future	• See myself has having the future I desire
• Set a plan for how to get there in 5 years	• Looking backwards to review the steps I took to get to where I am
• Adjust plan when circumstances get in the way	

This is empowerment in motion. We continue to take the steps we can take. On day one of our start-up business we have a defined vision and we employ this approach. However, as we build the business, we see new opportunities, and we may choose to include those in our vision because they also align with our investor, business customers, and social cause values in our value chain. These additions are not added lightly, since that level of alignment is rare. So, we now reset our internal GPS system to the new vision and look backwards to see if there are new steps that we need to take to get to the new destination. This is how it works once it is properly set forth and how we adjust, expand, and evolve our vision over time as we see new opportunities, we could not see the day we picked up this book.

Karma Applied to our Business Relationships

The essence of value creation is understanding what your avatar customer values. As we grow in our careers and expertise, we can lose sight of this if we are not careful. As our business grows, we need a variety of leadership skills and behaviors to see how all dimensions of a business work in harmony to provide that value. We may be tempted to believe that we have all the answers, but the key to empowering our business relationships is really in asking ourselves and our team the right questions and listening to their responses.

When we are looking to hire a vendor for their product or services, we know to ask about the attributes of the product or service, the service level agreements, terms and conditions, and the price. However, a relationship is not a single or even series of transactions. It is moving past the sales script and negotiating great terms and conditions. It is about understanding the vendors strategic vision for their product and company.

I worked with a naturopath who recommended a particular brand of supplements because of her deep knowledge of their policies for sourcing and development of the product. While she makes a commission on the products she resells, she also had done her homework. She researched other products and their manufacturing processes before she decided to work with this supplier. In the process of doing the research, she also developed a relationship with the business leader who formulates the product. He is now a source of information for her, for example when she is seeing a new patient with a different set of symptoms, she looks to develop a regime of supplements that will support her other modalities of providing treatment. This makes her valuable to her clients as they proceed on their health and wellness journey.

Tracking successes

It is clear in the first example that for a 15-month project, you need a plan with defined milestones, touch points across all of the thousands of employees impacted by the project and with the vendors to manage the circumstances and situations that arise, and develop a joint mindset and belief that they are on track to see the project to its successful conclusion. The plan has a cadence of meetings, communications, and action items that are assigned across the project and business leadership with the single aim of a successful project.

It is no less important for the second example to establish a cadence of accountability. In this example, there are two sets of success tracking that are needed. The first is between the naturopath and her supplement vendor. She may request reports of variations in the formulation that arise as a result of her vendors supply chain. She may also request advance notice of supply chain interruptions. This empowers her to build up a supply of products that are subject to volatility and also establish a broadcast email to her clients when a shortage or interruption is anticipated so they can modify their orders accordingly. This monitoring has several benefits. First, she has a steady stream of revenue from the supplements and second, it builds trust between her and her clients so they can be secure in knowing that their health won't be subject to the ups and downs of her vendor's supply chain. It also establishes credibility and integrity, showing that she values the business of her clients and her investment in their long-term healthcare results.

In my experience, many of us in the healing or social impact business do not take the time and discipline to establish these accountability metrics. The patient does not come back, they must be healed. We donate to a cause; it must make an impact. This is flawed thinking. In the first example, there are a variety of reasons a patient does not come back. They may in fact be healed, they may not have been healed and didn't feel valued or heard and went to find an alternate provider, their condition may have worsened and they are off to more critical care modalities, or in extreme cases, they didn't recover and have transitioned on to another dimension.

In the second example, our contribution may have gone into a general pool for overhead, it may make a ripple, or it may make a splash. Without reading the reports of the cause you contributed to, you do not have the knowledge or belief that your donation made an impact. Doing your research is just one dimension of building a relationship with the cause you are supporting. You may expand the relationship by subscribing and following the social media posts, attending events, and participating in their cause directly in a role that fits your time and talents. By tracking your dollars, time, and their progress as a cause, you can track the success that you contributed to and are a part of creating.

Develop New Leaders

Lifting as we climb is the most effective form of empowerment for us as leaders. Our goal is to create the next generation of leaders, not just a count of followers. If you are a solopreneur, you create your team of individual relationships to lift and grow in success together. This can be done in a variety of ways, beyond the example of empowering our business relationships with our vendors and suppliers. It can be accomplished by participating in the local Chamber of Commerce, Meetups, and other networking venues, or mentoring junior leaders in the organization of your cause or community.

Skin in the Game Is the Best Way to Boost Employee Retention – I have a client whose business started with 13 shareholders. Over the past year we have added a few select other leaders who also are shareholders. Each one is a worker who earns dividends based on profits. Not only does this create a relationship between owners and team members, but it keeps everyone focused on what matters. The owner does not have to worry as much about workers' desire to improve performance: Those who understand they are actively creating income naturally want to create company value.

We have heard about the value of employee engagement — high engagement prevails as the best indicator of performance. Offering ownership in the company gives employees a reason to feel tied in and engaged for the long haul. By providing a profit-sharing program, we attract talented people who understand and value the concept of ownership and collaboration.

Aside from naturally changing the tenor of the workplace from a group of self-interested individuals into an efficient, driven team, ownership gives staff members an opportunity to peek into profit and expenses. This insight helps them realize how important their expertise is, no matter what their positions.

To avoid retention issues from the beginning, this can be incorporated into the startup business model as noted in the earlier example. However, if you have tried incentivizing employees in different methods, such as bonuses or other benefits, to stick around and still see them dropping like flies, consider offering an ownership stake in your business. Here are some strategies to get started.

Create a profit-based bonus plan for all staff - If we work in a firm that has a bonus plan for both hourly and salaried staff based on meeting individual quotas or bringing in new hires, make a change. Switch the bonuses to the profitability of the company overall. Outline your profit plan very specifically so workers know what to expect and how they can earn more money. The key may be in realigning existing performance metrics to coincide with the new desired behaviors.

Remember to stay fair and consistent with your plan. Otherwise, the incentive will seem arbitrary, and people will lose interest in contributing to the collective good. Note that some individually motivated staff will wean themselves initially, but you can recruit and hire new employees more in alignment with this strategy.

Set up stock acquisition, if possible - Employee stock options allow you to keep ownership within your ranks. When employees who own stock leave our company, we buy back the shares. This means that the team members who are driving the company to success will be the ones to reap the advantages of the good years. Plus, stock ownership makes exceptional team members more apt to plant roots because their shared equity anchors them to the brand. Our personnel see themselves not as single players but as part of a productive group responsible for the company's reputation and growth.

Encourage active participation - Give our employee stock options that make them essentially employee-owners. Some companies then use that role to create the opportunity for more involvement by asking them to help run the company in a variety of ways. Staff representing management, sales, administration, and compliance have all joined forces to serve on committees, be part of task forces, and join the board.

This is optional, of course. Yet it opens the door for people to feel heard and respected. In addition, workers blame management much less frequently because they know the buck stops with them. We see new behaviors such as voluntarily shutting off the lights, picking up trash in the parking lot, or mentoring colleagues just because it made sense for the organization's health and viability.

Many types of incentives work in the short term, but an ownership stake reduces friction and increases momentum over the long haul. Give your employees more than a reason to stick around—motivate them to go the extra mile. Then, sit back and watch in wonder as your team makes some profitable music.

Mentor relationships are essential to leadership empowerment. Every leader needs a mentor and my vision is for every leader to be a mentor too. There are structured mentor/protégé programs that you can participate in or you can cultivate your own mentor/protégé relationship.

I had the amazing opportunity to participate in and grow thank to the national leader for my firm's Diversity and Inclusion mentorship program. We held an annual kickoff that confirmed existing and new mentor/protégé relationships through a matching algorithm. We held a series of monthly meetings for the entire group on a key topic or theme bringing in accomplished leaders from within our firm or others to deliver the program. The mentor and protégé pairing then also established their own cadence. It is the protégé that drives the scheduling, topics, and preparation for the meetings.

To track the impact of the program, we measured retention of employees over a three-year period as well as participant surveys on the programs. Our main goal was to increase retention of our diverse employees as they create value in bringing their authentic selves to work each day and feeling valued enough to stay. The program increased retention by 33% over the course of the three years, which I know because I was in a position to monitor its effectiveness. Participation also grew by 100% over that same period. Knowing this is important to me, not just as a line on my resume or in this book, but because the time, effort, and actions I took resulted in measurable, tangible value to others.

A board can play a role in mentoring the CEO. However, if there are still signs that the CEO is struggling, they can ask for additional resources to divide the workload according to capabilities and business needs. Another option is an executive coach. A great coach will help the CEO develop the skills needed to manage the company through rapid growth and change.

The majority of early stage CEOs do not have executive coaches, but those who do report that they receive real value from the relationship. A coach is a safe place to get unvarnished feedback without the risk of divulging problems that might result in the CEO losing his/her job or harming key personal relationships.

Great coaches do not come cheap and so many early stage companies expect one of the board directors to take on this role in the early days. This can work, but is not ideal, due to the issue surrounding confidentiality. However, it can be useful during an interim time period where an outside coach is not within your budget. Everyone can benefit from some outside perspective and guidance. Whether you are working with a first time CEO or an experienced serial entrepreneur, an executive coach is a resource we should look to retain.

There are other times where additional resources help out. During my weekly conversation with a CEO, he started the call with a brief status update on the past week. Most of the update focused on the myriad tasks he had to deal with in the past few days. I was taken aback by the amount of time he was spending on low-level administrative tasks. When he finished his update, I asked one simple question. "Do you enjoy doing those tasks?"

His response was very telling. "No, I hate doing this stuff, and I'm not particularly good at it! I know it takes me more time than it should, but there is no one in the company who I can pass it off to". At the time of this conversation, the company had about seven employees, and they were generating a small amount of revenue from a handful of customers. As you can imagine, resources were pretty tight.

My second question to the CEO was, "Why don't you hire an executive assistant or executive administrator? That person could take over all these tasks you do not like, and you could put your time and energy into more valuable efforts for the company". The phone went quiet for a minute or two, and then he responded. "That's a good idea, but I don't think we can afford that hire".

He was right in one way. The company did not have a lot of money to spend on this type of resource. But he was wrong in another: what the company really could not afford was to not have a CEO, or rather to have a CEO spending all of his time on non-essential things.

In the end, I prevailed and convinced him that this investment in growth was the right thing to do. He was letting the minutiae of running the company keep him from addressing more important items. A few months after hiring his assistant, I noticed during our weekly phone calls that the CEO was a bit more relaxed and on top of his main responsibilities. I felt good that I had helped him get out of his own way.

Burnout is for skeptics

Skeptics have a particular set of paradigms that are patterns of behavior. Thinking back to the pyramid in the preface, their belief system revolves around work is hard, work expands to fit available time, and if they cannot see me doing it, it does not count. There are other similar statements, but you get the point. Maybe we customarily choose to work for managers, rather than leaders, regardless of their position or title. Maybe it came from our parents who raised us with a strong work ethic. It really does not matter where it comes from, the goal is to recognize the signals that you are getting from buying into that set of behaviors. You may be a person who is gaining weight or otherwise experiencing a decline in vitality because you are choosing to work instead of exercise and eat well. You may have fallen into the habit of going to the bar or relying on pharmaceuticals to release the work, tension, and stress accumulated through the day. Your family and friends may be sending distress signals because you have put off spending time with them.

Changing our beliefs can be as straightforward as thinking about empowerment as a synonym for balance. No, straightforward and easy are not equivalent during the process of transformation, but the outcome does make life easier. Think about the acronym SPIRIT as we progress through this transformation process.

Single-threaded Focus – we have discussed vision and keeping it front and center as an organizing principle for your calendar, your activities in the calendar, and the prioritization of those tasks as life intervenes. You can apply this to how you lead as well. Impart your vision to your team and trust that they will come through. Teach them the importance of taking the top priorities and focusing on them and reporting back on progress and barriers. If we focus on the wildly important, not just the urgent, we win.

Purpose – each person on your team has a purpose. Find your own superpower. It is likely hidden to you because you are so in tune with it that you take it for granted. What do you do differently that surprises you when others do not see it? Ask your mentor or close friend, they may be more aware of it than you are, and it may be why they admire and respect you. Now that you know your own superpower, you can identify the gaps, or areas where you need support. This creates your team building and/or hiring strategy.

You hire the best and brightest, likely even more qualified than you in some aspects of their position. You want the best tax strategist that understands all the recent changes and nuances. Of 77,000 pages of IRS tax code, only 15,000 apply to those who are employees, the rest apply to business owners. Do not rely on one semester of accounting to see you through, hire the best and listen to their recommendations and reasoning. Let them achieve their purpose and demonstrate you value it by implementing their ideas. Not every idea is feasible in a moment's notice, but acknowledge the idea, why you thought it was valuable, and tell your entire team. They will respect that even if their idea did not make the cut, you are open to good ideas.

Intention – being clear about your intentions and the intention of the business creates clarity. The system with the least diversity yields results the quickest. If you can instill your intention for your day, week, month, or year in your team, they do not need to spend cycles asking for clarification, direction, etc. Take a few extra minutes to really connect the dots and give the full direction up-front and keep meetings brief and on topic so your team fully engages, and their attention does not wander.

Recognition – tie the performance measures to the intention and vision. Amazon only has four performance measures across their enterprise. This way they do not get into competition across divisions, lines of business, or leaders. The measures should reflect realistic targets that can be achieved in a 40-hour work week. Meet regularly to tell your team where they stand and give constructive feedback. Recognition is also tangible and discussed in the earlier part of this chapter.

Inspiration – think of a game you love, Fortnight, Candy Crush, etc. What is it about that game, over all the others that may be on your device draws you in? Find your inspiration factor for your business. It may be different for employees versus clients. Then market that inspiration to each audience. For employees it begins in the recruiting stage and continues through to creating a culture that means employees for life. You want your employees that move on to speak well of you and your business. Create an alumni association as well as a culture that values each person on your team every day. This is your way to create the same affinity and loyalty with your clients. Encourage them to follow you on social media and create contacts in your CRM system with tags that recognize how they found you and why they stay. Do the market research and validate your ability to keep them inspired. Disney is an expert at this, they retain the stickiness of the classics like Cinderella and Snow White, while expanding into new frontiers with Star Wars.

Talent – during that hiring and recognition process, demonstrate value by seeking talent that is aligned to their purpose. If they are just in it for the paycheck, you will have a harder time with turnover and retention. The cost of acquisition and onboarding of a new employee is far greater than the cost of paying a fair market wage and designing compensation packages that reward both individual and team performance.

The outcome of adopting the SPIRIT approach is that you build an aligned and empowered team. This allows you to have time to step back out of the tactics and focus on strategy and alignment with the vision and to see where the vision can be expanded, evolved, and extended. It allows for time to be curious and explore new perspectives and not make each day a repetition of the previous day. This ability to think instead of following a pattern brings both personal and company growth.

Understanding and Leveraging Our Board of Directors

Being CEO can be one of the loneliest jobs in the world. As CEO, you are ultimately held accountable for the success or failure of the company. Our employees and their families depend on us for their income. Customers depend on us to solve important problems for them. Shareholders depend on us to deliver the promised return on investment. When times are good and the company is growing and profitable, it is a great job to have. Unfortunately, times are not always good. No company I have ever been involved with for a decent length of time avoided having serious issues crop up that the CEO had to address quickly. Businesses are complex organisms. Primarily, this is due to the fact that all businesses involve people... and people are the root cause of most problems.

We might think that the CEO can rely on their senior managers to deal with complex issues. In many large organizations they can most of the time. Even in big organizations, senior managers have the luxury of reaching out to their peers and the CEO for help. The startup CEO does not have a peer at the company and often does not have a full set of capable senior managers to help shoulder the load. The CEO must reach out to the board for guidance.

As a director, it is their responsibility to help the CEO through these difficult moments. It might be a conflict with a co-founder that will result in a breakup of the founding team. Or it might be a difficult strategic decision that results in a layoff of half the staff. Whatever the situation is, directors need to act like a head coach, a chief psychologist, or a consigliere. And providing that kind of help requires being involved and having a good relationship with the CEO.

Before a CEO is comfortable asking for help from a director, there needs to be a strong personal relationship. That relationship must be built. Before initiating an offer to join a board, the CEO and director get together in a social setting. It might be dinner or perhaps a sporting event, or even joining them on a customer call during a quiet moment. Whatever the setting, the purpose of this time is to get to know one another in a non-work-related context. The goal is to understand each other's personal motivations. That can take some time and often requires interaction outside the conference room.

Once the director joins the board, as CEO we should have an approach that works well. A 30-60-minute phone call into his or her calendar at a scheduled time every week. This should be a meeting the CEO and the director prepare in advance. There are obviously times where a call needs to be canceled. But in a typical year, the CEO and director will end up talking at least 40 times. On my weekly phone updates with the CEO, I like to keep it really simple. I start by asking for a quick status update on the business, but I do not dig into the nitty-gritty of the company's daily operations. I spend most of my time discussing the following three themes: Team, Finances, and Strategy. To build a relationship during the calls, this involves asking a few unobtrusive questions that are related to the CEO's and director's personal lives. The goal is understanding primary non-work interests: family, health, and hobbies. This is all part of breaking down barriers and allowing the CEO and director to build a position of trust and familiarity. They cannot help each other if they do not build real, deep comfort and trust in our relationship.

When talking about the "Team", a director wants to make sure the CEO is spending a significant percentage of their time hiring the right people ("A" players), building a strong company culture, and keeping the organization focused. In our weekly conversations, they are always listening for bottlenecks that might indicate it is time to bring on a new team member or create a new role. Sometimes it is as simple as hiring an assistant to offload some of the non-critical tasks on the CEO's overburdened desk. Other times it is when the company reaches an inflection point where it is important to bring on a full-time CFO to make sure the company is receiving the right metrics to help operate and grow the business. The conversation about Team is the most frequent topic on a weekly CEO call.

With "Finances", the key topic revolves around not running out of the financial resources necessary to invest in the company's growth. Startups burn through cash quickly. The biggest mistake a board and CEO make are to not be prepared for replenishing the bank account in time. As a CEO, you need to make sure the director is confident that you recognize when the company will be out of cash and the steps you are taking to keep that from occurring. Conversations around Finances are episodic. They are held frequently during periods of fundraising, and then they go quiet for a quarter or two when the company's bank account has sufficient cash to last the year.

The final topic, "Strategy", is a bit more nuanced. The strategic vision is the source for alignment across the entire organization, We as CEOs are responsible for setting the vision and communicating progress and adjustments as the company strategy expands over time. This is an important aspect of company culture. A director can help the CEO by acting as a sounding board in defining and refining the company strategy. Conversations on strategy occur on a fairly regular basis.

Delivering Impact

Between 2001 and 2012 my role in consulting was in working with public water authorities to enable their strategies for maintaining their infrastructure while enabling conservation and sustainability strategies for our publicly delivered water supply. It was important and amazing work. During that time, I worked with a city agency in Texas that was on the border between rain and drought conditions every year, alternating how they would manage supply. The complication for them was that they experienced a large population growth and new developments and permits were needed as well as the potential for expansion of their infrastructure and capacity.

The CEO and his leadership team from across 12 lines of business came together to develop a large-scale transformation program that had six component projects within its scope. They were looking to an integrated solution for Finance, Human Resources, Revenue Billing, Enterprise Assets, Permitting, and GIS systems that all worked together to assign work, process transactions, and build a robust staff. Each component project empowered a piece of the business, yet the program as a whole would propel the organization to a new level to handle not just the day-to-day business of delivering clean water to every constituent, but would also advance their overarching strategy of reducing water consumption through conservation and not losing revenue by constituents pay less because they used less.

When the project was complete, all of the executives were happy and felt as though their objectives were met. However, two years later, the city and surrounding area were hit by a drought that was larger and longer in duration than forecasted. I reached out and spoke with their COO after reading an article in *USA Today* that was front page news on how their long-term vision and strategic and operational execution meant that despite the exceptionally harsh conditions they were facing, the water system was up to the task in providing a consistent supply of clean water and in enforcing the drought restrictions in place to the benefit of the entire community.

This is the type of leadership we want to embody as we build and grow our businesses. We design a bold, far-reaching strategy and then take the actions and measure the impact to see that we are on track for attaining that vision.

Giving Back to Our Community

As a social business entrepreneur, we have an amazing opportunity to give back to our own communities. Sometimes we focus on solving larger societal impacts such as climate change, food insecurity, and particular health causes, and we do not always make the linkage back to the impacts we see in our own community.

Building a technology or other product or service that has global or other large-scale reach is incredibly important and unless you've already put in place some of the ideas for boundaries, using your calendar as a tool for a full spectrum life and other concepts, it may seem daunting to add another philanthropic activity to your calendar. Here is why you should.

Benefitting your community is always a great idea. Other than your business, your home is likely your greatest asset. Making your community stronger is a great way to protect that investment. Volunteering your talents at the school increases the reputation of the school and gives the children a greater connection to how the materials they are reading and topics they are learning will help them to be successful. The same principles apply to other community-based activities such as Boys and Girls Club, Habitat for Humanity, United Way, church, and faith-based initiatives to name just a few.

Benefit your business by your giving back. Congruence in our actions across our business and personal lives matters when you build a relationship with your clients. They see integrity rather than an opportunistic motive for your social business. In addition, we make great connections that expand our reach. We find new customers and new vendors, which lead to extraordinary opportunities to grow our business as we align with our target customers in all of our actions.

We can sponsor events that provide direct and passive marketing opportunities for our business or we can show up personally and build relationships by volunteering, serving on a board, or participating in other activities aligned to your purpose and talents.

Benefit yourself by the sense of gratitude that fills us with these efforts. We feel a great sense of accomplishment when we can improve the quality of life for the people we service through our efforts. We also increase our gratitude for not having to "walk a mile" in someone else's shoes and appreciate the blessings we have in our life that allows us to have the capacity for giving back. Infinite Intelligence is at work in guiding you to where your talents can best be used and how that aligns to your purpose.

CHAPTER SEVEN
EVOLVE

How We Evolve

The introductory picture to this chapter shows how the Slinky Dog has improved over time. We have that same capability. We come into this world with our DNA, which can be explained as a defined switchboard for who we are based on the genes provided by our parents. That is the nature side of who we are. However, like any switchboard, the decisions we make for ourselves create the story of our evolutionary journey. Our time in college, unless we were homeschooled, is often our first experience in self-determination and making choices about what we will focus our attention on learning and growing our capabilities into who we will become. Traditional K-12 education in the United States has a preplanned program of classes and maybe three tracks, special education, college preparation and a track with some exposure to the various trades via shop, architectural drawing, and other trade-oriented classes to round out the basic requirements for graduation. Some schools offer advanced placement courses in wealthier school districts. My desired school and desired career path did not mesh. I wanted to go to a particular school, but it did not offer a track for architecture. I majored in civil engineering at the beginning of my time on campus. The courses were challenging but not overwhelming. What was overwhelming was finding out what it was going to be like on a day-to-day basis with a career in that major. No one in my family had ever been to college, let alone become an engineer. My professors were great, but they had lived their careers as academicians. There was not internet yet, so the library was my path to research, and it told me a lot about the academics of engineering and the course of study, but not what was involved in working for an engineering firm. Finally, I gave up because I could not see a clear vision of what my life would be as an engineer, so I switched majors to business. I knew what businesspeople did. I had gone to the office with my father and had that example that I could put in focus. Despite the fact that I did not like the classes and material I was studying, that picture of how I would earn a living carried me through getting my degree.

We also evolve in other ways. One is being explored through science in the fields of epigenetics, nutrigenomics, and quantum physics to explain the age-old debate of nature versus nurture. Then we look at our own journey to see why this is important as we make our decisions moving forward. We will explore the evolution during our formative years and how we arrived at the decision to become exponential leaders and how that memory can be used to fuel our imagination for the future instead of terrorizing ourselves through second guessing. We can chose to nurture ourselves as adults and we explore what this looks like by the different leadership types to see where we naturally fall and where we can choose to round out our capabilities and/or design better business and other relationships by understanding how our perspective of each leadership type can inform our responses. We then move into the decisions we make and actions we take in each domain; health and wellness, business and philanthropy, relationships, and time and money freedom to explore our self-leadership capabilities and how we evolve into living a full spectrum life.

The Science Behind the Scenes

One field that is relatively new is epigenetics. I found a good short definition in *Psychology Today*.

"It used to be thought that we were born with a fixed genetic blueprint that determined our traits, behaviors, and health. Now, discoveries in the field of 'epigenetics' have radically rebooted this theory by demonstrating that our DNA is more of a switchboard than a blueprint. Epigenetics is the study of how external forces, such as our environment and life experiences, trigger on-off mechanisms on the genetic switchboard. Epigenetic scientists are examining the mechanisms by which genes become expressed or silenced with the goal of understanding how we can influence their activity and change our genetic health outcomes".

New fields in science are trying to understand the nature vs. nurture debate. How do our decisions and environment play a role on how we become who we are today? It encompasses a whole host of variables, which is why the progress is slow. Take for example identical twins. They start out with as close to 'identical' makeup as human beings can have, yet we see a different host of personality and behavioral and health expressions over time. One may have been treated differently by their parents than the other. One may play a musical instrument and the other may be athletic.

Another emerging field is nutrigenomics. Rhonda Perciavalle Patrick, Ph.D. is affiliated with Children's Hospital Oakland Research Institute and provides this brief definition "Our genes influence the way we absorb and metabolize micronutrients. Nutrigenomics looks at the influence genetic variation has over micronutrient absorption/metabolism and the biological consequences of this dynamic relationship. Our diet also influences which of these genes are turned on or off. Emerging evidence in the field of epigenetics has demonstrated that not only can we change the expression of our own genes within our own lifetime; sometimes these changes are heritable and affect our children and grandchildren. Her work focuses on exploring the intersection between genetics, nutrition, and environment: how our diet, micronutrients, exercise, heat stress, and sleep can change the expression of our genes and how this has profound effects on the way our body functions and ages."

In *Science Direct* under the section Green Chemistry - An Inclusive Approach 2018, Pages 109-128, this paragraph jumped out at me, "Some of the environmental chemicals may not cause DNA damage directly; they can cause epigenetic changes. This means that the DNA base sequence is not altered but the base is chemically modified so that the genetic information is expressed in a manner abnormal to correct cellular function. Moreover, it has become evident that posttranslational modifications of proteins associated with DNA (e.g., histones) can also lead to mutation via incorrect regulation of gene expression. Results of contemporary studies on animals (including humans) have also indicated that epigenetic changes can occur in response to environmental distress (e.g., famine, toxic chemicals) and cause an ailment(s) in the individual due to altered gene expression, and that these epigenetic changes, altered gene expressions, and ailment(s) are passed on to at least two and maybe three generations of offspring. The gene sequence, however, remains unchanged! This is referred to as transgenerational inheritance".

Quantum Physics has found one key discovery, that the smallest particles behave differently when they are under observation. There is a study that showed how particles behaved one way when shot through a single slit and differently when shot through the same wall with an additional slit added. This became the wave theory. Next, they applied this in another scenario and the particles behaved completely different. This naturally confused them, so they decided to place a camera on the other side of the wall to see why the particles were behaving differently. The results shocked them even more! Under observation the particles formed a completely different pattern. This is called the observer effect.

Once discovered, it explains why string theory has been so elusive to pin down, yet also forms the basis of how we understand from a scientific perspective how the world we formed continues to evolve. The basic theory is that everything is formed from the composition of various strings of matter. The lower the vibration, the heavier the object, mountains vs. kites. As humans we are all strings of energy, vibrating at different frequencies to navigate and find our place in the world.

For those of us who want to learn more, another good starting place is the website for How Stuff Works.

Until these sciences emerged and gained traction between 2014 and now, we believed in the blueprint theory that led us to believe that our DNA is fixed during conception and does not change. Now that we know more, we can apply these concepts to how we became business innovation leaders and our choices as we evolve and grow.

Let us look at an image that demonstrates the science and how we can apply it to get the results we envision as we evolve.

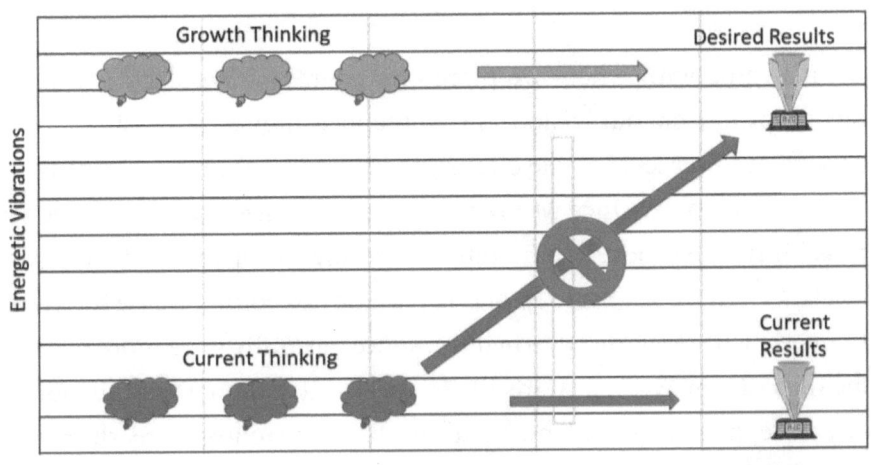

This Photo by Unknown Author is licensed under CC BY-NC-ND

This explains why any change we desire is difficult to achieve. We start an exercise or new eating pattern to improve our health, but we do not genuinely believe that we can attain the goal or that our actions are not enough to have influence. Without changing that cognitive behavior, we do not realize the results and we fault the actions or method used, rather than looking inward to change our belief to be a vibrational match for the object of our desire. This concept applies to any change we want to make. We make $250,000 per year and want to raise that to $1,000,000. How do we make that big of a leap to quadruple our income, we cannot work 4X as hard each day? We cannot get up and have the same thought pattern as the day before when we arrive at our desk for work. The diagram above illustrates that if we want elevated results, we need to elevate our thinking.

The next diagram illustrates how we go about implementing the formula to success using elevated thinking.

Attention → Thinking → Feelings → Actions → Results

It begins with where we place our attention. We decide to place our attention on our vision and value at a higher level rather than down at a lower level as the circumstance or situation is something we want to overcome. Once we are focused on the vision and value, we see possibilities that never came into our frame of reference at the lower levels. When we see more than one path or possibility, we instinctively know we will reach our destination, so we naturally have more positive feelings. Then we are more likely to act. It isn't a pass-fail option anymore, it is all about which path we like best to get there, the scenic way, the shortest way, the fewest turns, and failure isn't even an option, so we decide and get going. This leads to success. Just think about is. Say we are trying to get to the number eight. If you are just learning math and only see 0+8 and 1+7 as options, it can be pretty intimidating and may seem like all-or-nothing. But when you learn about more possibilities and see that 2+6, 3+5 and 4+4 get you there too, now you think, wow, there is no way to fail, I just have to get started. This formula helps us to understand the relationship between thoughts and behaviors and between the patterns of action and behaviors we put in place today and what is needed to reach and sustain the new level of performance.

Nature vs. Nurture

In our early years we start by making small decisions (do I want to be held, do I want a bedtime story, do I want a pacifier). Then, as we grow, we make more decisions about what we want to eat and wear and who we want to be around. As we learn we see more opportunities in who we want to be when we grow up and what specific games and sports we enjoy. Then we hit our teenage years and the decisions become more complex like who we are attracted to, what and who do we want to become, what activities, courses, and schools will help me accomplish my goals?

We may make other decisions that are not as overt and yet are still intentional. We may decide to go against advice we are given from a person we love and/or respect. Sometimes there is emotion attached to the decision that creates outright defiance or maybe they are small decisions such as when to come home or not doing my chores or homework.

When we make a choice for the first time, it feels different than when we make a choice to repeat something that worked before. Sometimes repetition brings safety and security. Other times it brings adrenaline.

At a point, the repetition becomes a habit. While habits have a bad name in general, some are quite good and useful and do not need to be challenged because they do not hold back our growth. Brushing our teeth frequently and looking both ways at an intersection before entering traffic or crossing the road are examples of those beneficial habits.

There are habits that serve their purpose for a time. For me one of those habits was making friends with older children rather than children of my own age. It reduced competition, provided better conversations, and helped support my voracious need to learn more. Yet, my senior year in high school, that habit became a roadblock. All of my friends were off to a variety of different universities and I had created a void in not having any friends in my grade level. This required me to grow. I reduced my course work since I needed very few courses to graduate and took on a job to earn money for college. I also invested time in younger students and helped mentor them. Other strategies were becoming the sports editor of the school newspaper, joining the yearbook team, competing in forensics, and debating in tournaments at a state level versus just the traditional competition.

Other habits are self-defeating. We begin to smoke or vape because others do it and we go to parties and learn to overindulge in a variety of these type of behaviors such as underage drinking and drug experimentation. Even if they serve a good function in helping us feel that we fit in, these habits become damaging when they are compounded into a habit.

Self-leadership is about recognizing when a habit is no longer serving us and taking the actions to evolve and grow in a healthy and authentic way. In my example earlier, it was easy to make good choices because they were not earth-shattering or ground-breaking changes. I did not face resistance from my parents and teachers. Instead they reached out and supported those choices. Yet, when it came to the ripple effects of taking a full-time job, versus a part-time job, the change was not entirely positive. Yes, I did accomplish my goal in earning money for college, but it came at a cost. My co-workers by and large never went to college and were into drinking, partying, etc. None of my previous friends were like that so I had new choices to make. I could become liked and a part of the group or stick with my previous choices and path. Working on sales commission, I earned good money. I spent some of it wisely like replacing our broken TV set at home with a better version. I also used my discount to buy a great stereo system (yes, I am that old) for my dorm room and other small appliances and devices that would be valuable in school. However, working from 1 – 9 PM came with the temptation to spend money on other less investment type purchases. We may choose to ignore those indicators or decide to be a victim and not rise above the challenges we face in serving our highest good.

Evolutionary Choices We Make as an Adult

As an accountant, I readily taught myself how to use an integrated financial software as a customer and then was a part of a project that exposed me to how the business rules were defined in the software. Soon, everyone was lined up at my desk asking situational questions on how to use the software to execute complicated, unusual transactions. This led to leaving my company and becoming a consultant. From a knowledge perspective, it was a seamless transition; however, my team noticed that in a different setting, when I needed to reach out to people, rather than having them line up to see me, I wasn't as confident as I needed to be. Fortunately, through a combination of feedback, experiences, and decisions I made, I stepped up and then began to rapidly progress in my client feedback and team evaluations.

As part of that evolution, I became more interested in how I could help my clients get more from the technology. Having held a senior level position in my previous company, collaborating with them to define their business strategy and new business processes was a natural extension. However, I began to identify internal conflicts within my customer executive leaders. While they were confident in all aspects of running their business, there was a wide variety of behaviors that demonstrated their anxiety about the system. Some were sure the technology would not work; others were concerned that their staff would not understand the new work patterns and/or how to use the system. This showed up in their unwillingness to communicate about the project and miss meetings where decisions were expected and/or other undesirable behaviors.

As a result, I became a founding member of our company's organization change management practice. We developed an approach based on leading practices focused on helping leaders guide their organization through the system and culture changes needed. Leaders responded enthusiastically to the service, others thought it was too ambiguous and longed for an exact science on how to do each step, while still others dismissed the value out of hand. Interestingly enough, the patterns of reactions were the same whether it was the reactions of leaders within my own firm or my customer leaders.

We choose day-by-day how we do or do not evolve. We make a choice to meditate and raise our belief each morning and plan for success, or we race around the house in a daily whirlwind that gets us and our family out the door, but off to a rushed and anxious start to the day. Once at work, we accept every meeting invitation, rather than stepping up and letting the meeting leader know we are already booked or even double-booked at that time. This creates stress by carrying the burden of knowing we are disrespecting the person by ignoring the fact that we can't make the meeting, or we create distrust by attending parts of two meetings and not getting the full picture, since our attention is distracted.

We can choose to invest in our team to prepare them to lead in situations where we have a conflict in our schedule, or we can reschedule the meeting for a time when we can fully participate. You will know whether it was just a one-off time where everyone wanted a piece of you at the same time, but overall your workload is manageable or if this is a pattern that is emerging and a signal that you are becoming a bottleneck, not an enabling leader. In the example above when you wanted to quadruple your income, it would be wise to assume that you are becoming the bottleneck and to achieve your desired results, you need to evolve how you delegate work. There are other fine-tuning actions that can be taken too. Are the meetings necessary, are they organized and productive, and are they the right duration to build the team culture and get to the point?

Implementing a calendar that is a supportive structure for growth and focuses on the actions that propel you forward, rather than a source of stress and anxiety, is essential in evolving your effectiveness in gaining your desired results. The other structure of support that is essential is finding a mentor. Continuing with the 4X growth pattern, the mentor you select should have a proven track record in earning and sustaining at least your minimum target level. They cannot provide advice if they have not achieved that level of thinking and performance. This is why many famous athletes become coaches; they have walked the walk and are sought after for their insights. Aiming too high at first may also be a mistake for a mentor. Bill Gates may not fully be in touch with the memories of how we he grew from startup business to a small business now that he has sustained a decidedly larger income stream for years. An executive from his firm may be a better choice at this stage of your growth pattern. We want to remain in our growth curve and not slip into the overwhelm zone by taking on too much at one leap.

Behavioral Patterns by Leadership Type

In the first chapter we discussed innovation leadership types. Futurist, Innovator, Technologist, and Humanitarian. Let us look at how we can make decisions starting today that will enhance our dominant leadership type effectiveness and grow and evolve our capabilities in the other areas. We also introduced the concept of the four dimensions to respect as small business owners. Let us take a look at how each leadership type may respond to these highlights from science.

Futurists may not get to this part of the chapter for a while. Putting on that hat, we may have been thrilled to explore an earlier topic in greater detail (e.g. the work on epigenetics, nutrigenomics, and quantum physics) to draw our own conclusions. Now that we are re-engaged, we can see that in a world of instant gratification, there are long-term consequences to simple decision we make every day that contribute to extending our health and vitality or enhancing the aging process.

We may also be seeing the results in our own stressful lives. We may be wondering about the impact of stress on our health, our business decisions, our sleep, and our relationships, but these decisions may be more tolerable for some people. We may be considering the impacts of short bursts of stress versus long-term sustained stress.

The choices we make at every meal, every meeting, and every relationship interaction add up over time. Like a savings account or other investment, the interest compounds and we create wealth. Futurists are most likely to immediately understand the long game involved in making healthy choices every day. Understanding the science behind accumulated decisions that form a pattern and change the direction of our very DNA, as well as our life's trajectory, is powerful to a futurist as it affects our business, relationships, and health for decades.

Innovators may have been a bit frustrated by what seems to be a never-ending list of future implications. They want to take the idea they identified and start thinking about how to formulate the idea into some sort of actionable concept. We are yearning to start the customer needs research and quantify the potential demand. We want to understand more about the problems people are experiencing and what patterns and trends are emerging.

We as innovators are tempted to skip to the fourth section of this chapter to start capturing and building the big into form. My invitation is to hold off and stay with the chapter as structured because as business leaders, we need to wear all of the hats at one time or another and we need to understand all of the facets of who we are as leaders to move fluidly when asked to wear different hats.

Technologists may already be mentally designing a new application, product, or service around these concepts. They may be skipping over what our customer may need or want and dive into solving a perceived technology problem related to this new information. They continue to add new cool features because they can imagine them. Not necessarily because anyone else wants them and that can be expensive. This is a prime factor in why new products do not launch or last. We get this new cool idea; it resonates with a current problem we have now or experienced recently. We take the next leap of logic and determine if I am experiencing this, others are too. While there is certainly truth in that statement, analysis and ideation are required to determine how many customers there will be, what issues they are facing, and how much it will cost to produce the product to determine the breakeven point. This often resonates as business overhead in the technologist's mind.

Humanists may have identified how this relates to their mission and purpose to serve. We are leaping to the big picture, is there a way to apply this knowledge to solving pervasive societal issues? We are taking the micro-science and applying this to large groups. If we understand how nurturing impacts our decisions, how can we change educational systems to head off biases that are introduced by teachers, or maybe how we can head off birth defects by educating doctors and women about the nutritional impacts during pregnancy. These and other ideas I did not think of are amazing possibilities. However, my invitation is to write down the big picture ideas and read on to see how to evolve our vision to incorporate those big picture ideas and work backwards to see how they can be put into action.

Regardless of what our dominant leadership type is, in order to take the next step in our evolution, it is all about identifying the choices we make and actions we can take. Likely we saw aspects of ourselves in each of the examples, since we are not paper cardboard caricatures, but multi-dimensional human beings.

Applying This to Our Future Vision

Here is where our vision for each aspect of the four dimensions starts to serve as a guiding light. Is our dream big enough to encompass all the dimensions and impacts the futurist in us has identified? Is our vision well-defined enough to help keep us on track as we make all these decisions? Let us review dimension by dimension to see how it plays out.

Health and wellness are the foundational dimension. It is where not everyone's vision will align at the higher level. Who does not want to be healthy, well, and vital? Yet, our actions are often in contrast to achieving this vision. We get in a hurry and stop at a drive-through for a quick meal or we go to the prepared food section of the grocery store instead of taking the time to look up recipes for home cooked meals when compiling our grocery list. Maybe we shop correctly, but then make the choice to eat out instead of cooking at home. Every day is a temptation to skip the workout, the meditation, to just take a walk, or park further away. We skip or do not really prepare for wellness visits with our healthcare provider. What different decisions are we willing to make to have the energy, vitality, mental clarity, and stamina to be effective business leaders?

If we are leading a small business, virtual or face-to-face, our health and wellness is the blood of the business. It can and should take many forms.

Mental clarity is essential in guiding our firm through the strategic and operational decisions that are presented every day. Our belief in our success is easiest, at least for me when I have effective strategies for managing stress.

Physical health is vital. Our leadership sets the direction, strategy, and culture for the business. One aspect is modelling the behaviors we desire in our team. Availability is also key; decisions require action within a short time frame. If we are out of commission, opportunities are missed. Time is another aspect, even if we have set up recurring processes and systems, there are a wide variety of actions needed in all aspects of our business every day. Energy and stamina are the other aspect that is important to our customers, business partners, and team notice when we are drained.

Mindset is a key component of wellness. If we believe, we achieve.

The Law of Vibration is the main law. It supersedes the more well-known Law of Attraction. Generating a state of core belief in our vision opens the mind to the actions we can take each hour, day, and week. It opens up the other mental faculties of imagination, memory, will, intuition, perspective, and reason. These are the key faculties we can leverage to overcome anxiety and fear when we abandon the habits that are no longer serving us and replace them with new actions that propel us forward.

Business and Philanthropy is the focal dimension of this book. We all lead different business ventures and going concerns. Identification of the capabilities we can grow and adopt are the key to driving success in small businesses. When we take the time to set up a scalable business model, marketing plan, and operational processes we can improve consistency of execution and evolve over time. Taking shortcuts is tempting but identifying the cost benefit of disposable processes and tools is important. It may be what is required in the short run, yet when making this choice a corresponding action should be scheduled for a future date to plan the transition from the disposable system, process, or tool to the replacement that will enable future evolution. More details on this dimension are revealed in each chapter of the book.

Relationships are how business grows and evolves. We will look at the impacts of how we evolve as leaders impacts our relationships with customers, business partners, employees, and our personal relationships.

Customers are required otherwise our business is an expensive hobby. The Law of Compensation identifies three aspects and the first aspect is need. Understanding our target customer is required to be able to understand in great detail the problem they are trying to solve and how our business fills that need. This understanding informs every decision we make as a leader. What makes our customer buy comes first, so that should be the basis of our marketing plan. Then the next step is understanding what makes them happy, which influences how we design our customer service. Understanding what prompts, them to refer our business grows our footprint and customer base. The net evolutionary step is capturing their feedback to evolve our product or service.

    Business Partners is a broad category for small businesses. Often, we rely on contracted services and products to build our business before we venture into hiring full or part-time staff. This is the key to innovation. Lone rangers and solopreneurs may start out as innovative. Then as the business grows, complexity emerges, and overseeing everything as a solo person has an opportunity cost that is related to the lack of available time to step back to think and dream. We may have the skills to prepare our own taxes, but are we missing out on time and knowledge that could be supplied by a CPA and/or Tax Strategist. We may also be able to track all of our transactions and invoices in a software application. That time spent instead of hiring a bookkeeper cost us opportunities to solve other problems or generate new ideas and value. Similarly, building our own website on Wix, Weebly, or GoDaddy may have been a great starting point, but it costs us opportunities in not having dedicated landing pages for offers and launches of new products or just having a more polished cohesive website. Marketing is a function that business leaders attempt to oversee themselves. Similarly, to the other functions, this may be a starting place that needs to be replaced with a business partner to attract more business in a sea of sameness OR to educate and differentiate why our innovation is the best fit.

    Time and Money Freedom is about what we do with the newly created time and money from our leadership decisions. It is not about just freeing up the time and money, as that does not provide the subconscious mind with the images needed to empower and sustain the new actions needed to generate the time and money.

    Time is a valuable commodity. My perspective is a bit different. For me time is about the present moment and being fully present at whatever I have selected for my needle-moving actions. As business leaders, we often define needle0moving actions only in the context of our business.

While this is essential and appropriate for a defined portion of our calendar, it is also appropriate to set aside blocks of time as needle movers to build out the other dimensions of our life. Relationships, health and wellness, and fun do not happen without attention and time. Think about our calendar as a structure of support. How do we organize our calendar in such a way that we prioritize each of these dimensions of a full spectrum life? Setting a lunch date with a friend, loved one, or business relationship secures that time on our calendar. When other opportunities come along, we can see our availability and avoid the stress of overbooking and double-booking by honoring the time we have set for these activities.

Money is our other valuable commodity. As with any other commodity, it is only valuable in how we use it to achieve what we would love that is right and good for all. While having assets in the bank provides a sound basis for loans, security, and retirement and is not to be discounted, in the present it is only valuable in how we can fund the needle-moving activities that make our lives worth living. Discerning how we spend our money and in what dimension of our life (relationships, business, philanthropy, health) can be freeing. It may sound counterintuitive to state that discernment is freeing. However, with discernment comes the knowledge that we are in tune with our inner guidance and there is no need to waste precious time and energy second guessing that decision. Investing in a vacation, wellness, business, or fun is just that, an investment not an expense. Using that justification for every little purchase is an excuse. That is why it is important to define what our vision for time and money freedom is and use that as our guideline in creating the conditions for discernment between investment and frivolous spending.

CHAPTER EIGHT
EVOKE

The Law of Vibration and Success

The introductory image evokes the thought of a Slinky® toy in our minds, without it actually being a Slinky®. We explored how applying scientific principles and a growth mindset can help us evolve our own self-leadership capabilities to raise our vibrations and become a match for what we desire. However, we also noted two important leadership principles, those being that we start with the end in mind and we lift as we climb. Once we are a vibrational match to our business goals, we make a greater impact when we evoke the same vibration from our team and create the culture of belief and attainment across our organization's structure. We move from simple math to exponential growth. That structure may be a series of outsourced and partnership relationships or it may be a staff of empowered employees to align around the business vision with the actions required to reach the success target we have defined.

Whole System Business Model

We discussed the development of an extensible business model in Chapter 3. For all businesses that continue to expand and evolve, they are a variety of variables to intentionally evoke to make the transition from one stage of business to another. We will look at each of these components to your business structure.

Community – for a social business impact is exponentially increased when building a community. Engaging with your customers to continue to tell the story of the impact you are making increases their engagement and support for both your business and your cause. Social media groups, meetups, and other networking events are great ways to establish a community. The other key component is featuring your three-year vision on your website and all of your marketing messages. This demonstrates your commitment to the cause and gives you an opportunity to interact with your customers by demonstrating value and not directly soliciting them for additional sales in every drop campaign.

Company Culture – having an intention culture of any kind is better than a muddled company culture. This is woven into your three-year vision and into all of your recruiting materials and messages. We also recommend incorporating culture questions into the interview and hiring process as part of how you set expectations during the onboarding process. Now that you have a core of committed staff at most levels, you can fine tune your recruiting as your vision expands and evolves. The other dimension as you move from solopreneur, who is a player coach, to the full-time coach and leader is to bring that core group and ideally all of your top-performing employees along with you as the business grows.

Today, there are a number of excellent tools that take care of employee feedback and engagement in an automated fashion. Programs that are lightweight and incredibly effective at gathering relevant information and presenting it in an actionable manner.

We need to incorporate continuous employee feedback into our companies and cultivate an environment for team members to thrive. The stronger the culture, the stronger the company. We are in control of our own culture. As business leaders in small businesses we want to be in alignment with the CEO culture to drive it through the organization.

Here are some additional ideas to strengthen culture:

Update your one-page strategic plan quarterly and use it as part of a quarterly all hands check-in. It will benefit everyone to understand how the performance goals and metrics align with the strategic vision. These may be done in an off-site retreat if you have a virtual office culture to stimulate the development of deeper relationships and engagement. The budget dollars saved in office space and infrastructure can be used to fund these efforts.

As part of maintaining your business structure, you are already conducting monthly meetings. As the business grows, we need to gauge when we move to more frequently held meetings and look at the agenda and effectiveness of the meeting facilitation to highlight not only our point of view and gain operational feedback, but to demonstrate how we value our leadership and support teams. Actively scheduling idea meetings for gathering new options for process efficiency, customer engagement, or product reliability are important to demonstrate that your team's input and ideas are not only valued but implemented to propel the business forward.

Depending on the scale and scope of your organization, you may want to have a weekly email blast or newsletter to all constituents: employees, advisors, mentors, and investors. Initially, the email should be pretty simple and then expand as the company grows and departments are formalized. This keeps everyone up to speed if they miss regularly scheduled meetings due to conflicts or absence. High-performing companies have high-performing cultures. Use these ideas to build a strong, enduring culture.

An energetic environment always starts with the people and their values. Here are some sample values from a well-known company.

Glass is Refillable - We always move forward. We work to understand the reality of the situation, then we make the decision to focus on the opportunities and fill our customer list and our open positions and align with our strategic vision.

Focus on Results – We understand what we are here to do and make decisions with purpose to achieve our goals. Employee visibility and busywork are distractions from our core values.

Bias Towards Action – We are motivated. We go out of our way to take the actions we can and source ideas that create new opportunities.

Values set the tone and aligned cultures have a magnetic energy. Corporate culture is intentional and powerful — make it the centerpiece of the company. Company culture down to its essence, describing it as a business's "operating system" that lets people do their best work. We as entrepreneurs must create a company culture we love, because one will eventually emerge no matter what.

Entrepreneurship – As entrepreneurs and business leaders, we see abundance in the world. An opportunity here, an opportunity there. This serves the entrepreneur well in the early days. We follow the process outlined in the Emerge chapter and get really great at identifying the customer's needs. The we rapidly flow through the incubation and funding process with the goal of earning a great product/market fit.

At some point, instead of chasing the next shiny object, it is time to focus. Instead of a default 'yes' it needs to be a default 'no.' This is hard for most entrepreneurs. Famously, when Steve Jobs returned to Apple after many years away, he killed off most of the product lines and reorganized the company around a limited number of initiatives. Focus becomes even harder when your startup is 'hot'. Everyone wants a piece of your time. We know we need to cultivate and retain relationships with our investors and that the media may start asking for interviews. As a social business, nonprofit organizations constantly ask for appearances and more impact. Ultimately, these are more distractions that can make focusing difficult.

The value of having built a great structure of support via tools like the calendar and activity and task tracking applications comes to the forefront here. Back to the original premise that you need to control your schedule, not have your schedule control you. Take a few minutes every

Sunday night and look at last week's schedule and the upcoming week's schedule. Retain you curiosity and energy by asking some basic, but difficult questions: What meetings were worthwhile? What meetings were not worthwhile? What are you excited about on the schedule? What aren't you excited about on the schedule?

Regularly take time to evaluate where effort is spent. Then, intentionally cut out the distractions. Not sure where to start? Compile a three-column list. What needs to continue? What needs to be delegated/outsourced? What needs to stop? Once you have your list, then add a task to address each of these actions. Keep the continue things on your calendar and schedule a meeting with your new delegate or outsourcing partner to make the handoff between what you are doing and what they need to add. Stop doing some things. You may need to start saying NO. This may be the hardest to do. Setting boundaries to guard your time, is often a necessary habit to protect our time for the things we value most. Saying no to participating in a good cause is not easy, but if that takes away time from other things that you value, then the decision does become easier. Keep in mind, just because it is hard, does not mean it is not the right thing to do. Shedding the comfort zone is the key to advancing to the growth zone.

Investing – Share the origin story of our business. Share our vision of the future. Share what is next for taking the actions to get us there. But, most importantly, do this in 100 words. Here's the value of maintaining your strategic one-page document, you keep it current and the action of working with it inside and out develops your capability to get to the heart of the matter and set ourselves apart. We are not working for a business; it is ours, we know every detail, if our facts or story resonate with an investor, they will ask us questions. The goal is to capture their interest then start building a relationship. How do all human beings do that? Through conversation. Talking at them endlessly does not demonstrate our knowledge, it demonstrates that we are not confident that we have a compelling vision and story. Keep it light, fun, and memorable. Stories are memorable, details are not. Take a few minutes, develop a simple pitch, a 100-word story, and align the team around it — think storytelling, not detail telling.

Let us flip the perspective for a bit and look at investing from the investor point of view. Understanding where they are coming from helps us to understand their motivation and circumstances and tailor our pitch to their needs, just as we would develop a strategy for a customer.

Today's standard startup funding model whereby entrepreneurs pitch angels, VCs, and family offices for money in exchange for preferred equity is mostly a challenged, broken process. Investors typically focus on distinct money regions. They also home in on business models that present a grand slam. They also refine their search to select startups that have the capital and revenue traction to generate significant growth rates. Even with that narrow focus, investing in startups is a great way to lose money.

The majority of angel investors I know have lost money investing in startups. Perhaps they are not good investors. Maybe they have joined a flawed network of investors that does not reach a diverse pool of entrepreneurs. Perhaps it is the entrepreneurs' problems (having a great idea but not understanding the difference between hypothetical valuation and hard dollars valuation). Regardless, this is not specific to a specific region. It is the same in all regions outside the money centers (Silicon Valley, NYC). Stories of investors writing a check for $25k to Uber and turning it into $100M permeate the media yet are so rare it is laughable. Only, it fuels the stories and desire for more people to become investors. One potential angel investor described it to me as wanting to spend 1% of his net worth on angel investing so that he could generate a new income stream and be less reliant on his day job. Unfortunately, the chance of that happening is slim to none. There is a perpetual cycle of regions trying to improve their local startup investing community. New angels come online and write some checks. They lose their money, and because of the poor outcome, will never do it again. Rinse and repeat each economic cycle.

THE SLINKY® EFFECT

Over the last few years, a new form of startup funding has emerged, but still represents a tiny part of the market, and it is known as revenue financing. Revenue financing is code for a loan that is paid back via a percentage of revenue. If the startup does better than expected, it is a super high interest loan. If the startup does as expected, it is a high interest loan. If the startup does worse than expected, it is a high interest loan paid back over a longer period of time.

Of course, a high interest loan requires the startup to pay back the debt, which takes cash away from growing the business. And, in the angel world, making 15% per year on the investment takes away the excitement and dream of making a 100x return. The future of startup funding outside the money regions should be a mixture of light revenue financing and traditional equity. Light revenue financing, such that the investor gets 1.2x of their money back in five years, keeps startup money flowing in the community. Traditional equity, such as the potential for a huge upside, keeps the imagination dreaming.

Angel investors are near the peak of this current cycle, and too much money is chasing too few high-quality deals, making it a great time to be an entrepreneur. Only this too will change — it always does. When angel investors come out of the next trough, and it's time to re-evaluate the startup funding model, a combination of returning capital to the investor community on a consistent basis and equity upside will result in a more sustainable and successful eco-system. Experts are recommending a structural change in startup funding to a mix of light revenue financing plus traditional equity to improve the startup world.

Early stage investments — primarily post-seed and Series A — are still quite limited. The number of investors that focus on this stage in the $750k – $3M in revenue range has not appreciably changed. Without expansion the number of startups that raise rounds in this stage has not changed. Investors at this stage often write checks that are larger than angels can put together, so it is not possible to bypass this funding source with more non-institutional money.

Seed/angel rounds are still the most challenging area. Just under 1,000,000 US entrepreneurs reached out with idea-stage startup ventures in the last half of 2018 to the first half of 2019. There are about 1,500 US based angel investor networks. Each network invests in 5-10 start ups per year. Local investors are still primarily wealthy people who did not make money in technology, and thus their appetite for startup investing is relatively low. To grow the angel community, we need to have more successful large startup exits to pay back the angel investor community. Today, there is a strong cohort of local growth stage startups valued in the hundreds of millions and a few in the billions. Once this wave of startups, typically 5-10 years old, reaches exit maturity, expect the local angel community to ramp up and hit a new high. To beat the odds, follow the advice in the Emerge chapter carefully, investors are looking for unicorn ventures that will beat the odds.

While the funding climate has not changed recently, the overall tenor of the startup community is humming along nicely. Look for the funding climate in the idea/seed stage to grow nicely in the next 3-5 years once we have a wave of big startup exits.

The common reasons raising venture capital is not right for most entrepreneurs boils down to exit strategy and the gap between hypothetical valuation and market valuation. The entrepreneur is on the clock from the time the investment is closed. They have a contractual exit strategy and it requires a 5x greater return during that period for the founder to make the same money.

Beyond the common reasons, the reality is that most entrepreneurs cannot raise venture capital because they do not have enough revenue traction, or truly exponential growth projections grounded in market validated terms, strong gross margins and profit possibility, and a huge market opportunity. The common thread noted by investors is that we as entrepreneurs spend time trying to raise institutional money when that time is better spent building the core business.

The solution: find a trusted advisor or mentor in the community to help think through financing options. Most of the time venture capital is not the right path and is not even an option due to the business characteristics. Entrepreneurs would do well to better understand venture capital and know that most of the time it does not make sense.

Last week I was talking to an entrepreneur that was dead set on raising venture capital. Naturally, I wanted to understand more and asked a number of questions. Turns out, this entrepreneur just thought it was the next step to being successful. Venture capital should not be viewed as just another step in the startup journey — raising venture capital is a serious decision that should not be taken lightly.

Here are several implications of raising venture capital:

Growth – Startups are growth-oriented organizations. Raising venture capital takes the emphasis on accelerated rather than organic growth and raises it to max — everything is focused on growth. If growth stalls, more money needs to be raised or the company needs to be merged with another company that is growing faster.

Timeline – As soon as you raise institutional capital, (as different from angel capital, family office capital, etc.) the business is now on a timeline to sell in as little as 3-5 years and as long as 7-10 years. No matter how you feel, the business has to be sold or go public, in an effort to generate returns for our limited partners, the people and institutions that provide capital to the venture capitalists.

Partnership – Selling a piece of equity is signing up for a long-term partnership with the investor. The relationship should be viewed as a partnership and not merely as an investment. Only raise money from investors you want to work with indefinitely. Think back to the notes on the role of our Board of Directors; for each board member, there is a director relationship to maintain and often they are your investors and have a stake in the results.

Funding - recently Atlanta companies raised $650M across 38 investments — the best Q2 ever — according to Pitch Book – NVCA Venture Monitor. While the amount of funding fluctuates on a quarter-by-quarter basis, setting a new high bar with our best quarter ever is an indicator of progress. Funding is only one piece of the puzzle, but it is an important one. Atlanta's startup community is making real progress and has much work to do.

Last week I was talking to an entrepreneur and the topic of the Atlanta startup community came up, specifically ideas to grow the community faster. Looking back over the last seven years, we've made substantial strides by adding Techstars Atlanta, Atlanta Tech Village, Backed by ATL, Engage, Atlanta Startup Village (14,000+ members!), several seed funds, two IPOs, four unicorns, and much more. Only, even with our continued success, there is a feeling we have not accelerated the growth of the overall community enough to reach the next level. As the region's leaders came together, they brainstormed what is missing, and several ideas came to mind:

Diversity and Inclusion - Programs like "Startup Runway" and "It Takes a Village" are helping address the diversity and inclusion challenges in the region but we need more, much more. Say there are 3-5 groups working on this for the startup community, we likely need at least 15-20 to make a big impact.

Angels - Looking at recent angel deals over the last 24 months, there are roughly 10 local angels that lead deals regularly (defined as 5+ deals historically). For everyone that will lead and put a deal together, there are another 10 that participate because they trust the lead. With 10 lead angels and 100 secondary angels, there are not that many regular angels. Many more startups raise angel money each year, but it is almost always from a first-time angel that is not a regular. We need at least 100 regular lead angels and 1,000 secondary angels — much work to be done.

Seed Funds - We have seen several local seed funds emerge including "Valor Ventures", "Knoll Ventures", and "Tech Square Labs" with a couple unannounced ones in the works. Seed funds are an important part of the community as they have committed capital that has to be deployed in a designated time period, as different from angels who might never do another deal. In addition, a strong seed fund community provides more support to angels helping them see a potential funding path forward, especially due to Series A rounds becoming what used to be Series B rounds. With 5-7 local seed funds today, we likely need 15-20 to achieve the next level of scale.

Startup Hubs – The Atlanta Tech Village is now seven years old and helped establish the startup center of gravity in Buckhead. The ATDC has been the startup hub in Midtown for decades. Downtown has the excellent Switchyards. Now, Atlanta is booming around the Beltline's East Side Trail and growth in the perimeter is robust, making both areas logical spots for more startup hubs.

Peer Connections - Atlanta is a very inviting, informal town for entrepreneurs. Groups like the Entrepreneurs' Organization and Young Presidents' Organization have strong local chapters. Only, there is a gap in peer connections for tech entrepreneurs to network with and learn from each other separately from the long-standing existing ones that focus on tech executives and service providers. The best example to emulate is Mindshare in Washington D.C.

Entrepreneur Education – From a founder's perspective with so many options and little organization due to the informal culture, navigation is a bit challenging. Where do you go next? Showing up at a startup hub and plugging into the community is likely the best answer. Only, it is a hodgepodge of events and programs, serving a variety of audiences. Investors would do well to create stronger programs geared directly towards helping tech entrepreneurs get going — bootcamps that cover the most important topics.

Storytelling - Easily the most nebulous, and possibly important, is how to tell the Atlanta startup ecosystem story better. There are many statistical B2B successes across MarTech, cyber security, FinTech, and health IT subsectors. Metrics and track records are excellent and appeal to the analytic side of our brains, whereas decisions are made with the emotional side of our brain. If you are an investor and sit in a room where startup after startup comes in and presents numbers, metrics, and statistics, the brain cannot absorb all of that data. What is needed is the combination - metrics, results, and a memorable picture. Think about it, when COVID first hit, the individual stories were compelling, then as we hit the 100,000 person death toll, it became a statistic, it became too large for a person to imagine, too impersonal to relate to, and people reverted back to old behaviors and the spread accelerated. Did that spur more action? No, what it did was change the story back to individual rights, because people could relate to their own struggle with restrictions and the scale was not large enough that it had hit their own family.

As we reach out to tell our story, we need to keep these principles in mind. Yes, we have to have facts and figures grounded in reality, but we also need to have a compelling story of how our business will change someone's life. We need to change the trajectory and carve out a path for the next generation of entrepreneurs. It is great that the investors have chosen to focus on B2B startups and it is their strength, yet the marketing has not been exciting or compelling as compared to Austin and Boulder, whose stories are mentioned regularly in the national press. The community is still struggling with how do to get Atlanta on those same lists for startups. This will attract high quality opportunities for investors.

What's Next - Atlanta has rapidly become a R&D hub for companies headquartered elsewhere and that serves a roll in recruiting talent to the region, but the real opportunity is growing the startup community with locally headquartered companies. Local startups invest more in the community, build greater wealth, and develop the next generation of entrepreneurs at a faster rate.

To get to the next level as a startup community, it is going to take a substantial number of new success stories, many more organizations helping a variety of entrepreneurs, and a greater level of local investment. Atlanta has the basis of the platform, and with hard work plus a little luck, will be able to get there in 5-10 years.

THE SLINKY® EFFECT

Funding Climate Outside the Money Regions - Whenever I talk to a startup person outside our region, (investor, journalist, etc.) they like to ask about the current funding climate in our region. Money is always a popular topic, especially when the economy is hot, and startups are the featured investment while the stock market is variable and bank investment returns are minimal. Only, the funding climate outside the money regions of California and New York has not appreciably changed in the last 2-3 years.

More money is sloshing around on the sidelines waiting to be put to work. Limited partners have huge commitments in funds and venture investors are trying to put the money to work. Yet, this is primarily for growth/later stage investments when the metrics are solid and it is clear the startup is going to win, it is simply a question of how much. For these growth/later stage investments, investors will travel. Distance is a pain but not that big a deal. If you can write a $50M check and underwrite a 3-5x return in 3-5 years, it is a pretty easy 'yes', especially if there is a direct flight (the money people still hate layovers).

Early stage investments — primarily post-seed and Series A — are still quite limited. The number of investors that focus on this stage between $750k – $3M range in revenue has not appreciably changed. Therefore, the number of startups that successfully raise rounds in this stage has not changed, and without more investors, the quantity of these types of funding will not increase. Investors at this stage often write checks that are larger than angels can put together, so it is not possible to bypass this funding source with more non-institutional money.

Seed/angel rounds are still the most challenging area. Idea stage startups are plentiful, but highly risk-loving capital is not. Local investors are still primarily wealthy people who did not make money in technology, and thus their appetite for startup investing is relatively low. To grow the angel community, we need to have larger amount of startup exits. Today, there is a strong cohort of local growth stage startups valued in the hundreds of millions and a few in the billions. Once this wave of startups, typically 5-10 years old, reaches exit maturity, expect the local angel community to ramp up and hit a new high.

While the funding climate has not changed recently, the overall tenor of the startup community is humming along nicely. Look for the funding climate in the idea/seed stage to grow nicely in the next 3-5 years once we have a wave of big startup exits.

Leadership – Recently I was talking to an entrepreneur that shared stories of a previous startup he had joined a few years back. The now-removed leader of this previous company had a big-shot corporate executive background and was placed in this over-funded startup before it had product/market fit. As expected, their office was lavishly furnished, money was spent like they were already a profitable cash cow, and six months later the startup was bankrupt. Boom, millions of dollars incinerated and nothing to show for it.

Starting lean and scrappy is an important part of the startup process. When entrepreneurs raise a large round before a repeatable, scalable business model, most of the time bad things happen. Entrepreneurs are an optimistic bunch, so it is only human nature to burn all the cash in 18 months, regardless of whether or not the business is working. When the cash is burned and the business does not make enough progress, investors are less likely to put in more cash, the cap table is often broken, and the startup usually ends in failure.

Mindset is the key to self-leadership. View your investors as partners in your business and focus on what you can do to be fiscally responsible. Most successful entrepreneurs tell tales of how they treated the company's money as their own, put it back in over and over to grow and scale the business, rather than to generate a lavish lifestyle. Every dollar we save is a dollar to invest and grow our business. Do not think it is only $20 here and $1500 for a business trip, think about what those dollars could do for product improvement, customer acquisition, or debt repayment. Little costs add up to big costs as the business scales.

Now, once the business model is working, there does come a time to ease up on the scrappiness — within reason, of course — and find a comfortable financial balance between spending too conservatively and being a spendthrift. But, like many things, as the financial purse strings are loosened, it becomes harder and harder to tighten them back.

Ego Management - At one of the events I attended, I listened to an amazing entrepreneur tell his story and it was incredibly compelling. Only, every 10th word was "I." "I grew sales 30% last quarter". "I acquired a competitor last year". "I hired an amazing executive". "I raised an institutional round". Finally, I interjected and asked, "Are you open to feedback?"

He was curious and I imagine he was considering what he had said was not necessarily feedback oriented. I shared that his use of "I" was disappointing. He did not achieve those things by himself. He leads a team, not just himself. Leaders need to say "we" and not "I", especially when referencing organizational results. "We" accomplished the goal. "We" made it happen. "We" > "I", always.

Leading as a Coach - The Gestalt Protocol, in its simplest form, says to share personal experiences for the purpose of giving advice only using 'I' and never 'You'. Most often, when people give personal advice based on their experiences, it is in the form of "You should do X because that's what worked for me". Instead, remove the use of 'You" and reword it with 'I' so that it is like "I did X and here's what I learned".

When giving advice, especially since we as business leaders and entrepreneurs are in a position of power or more experience, it's too easy to start telling the other person how to do things, even while we lack the details and context of the situation beyond what we've been told. In terms of effectiveness of our advice, not just for the specific advice but in sustaining a long-term relationship, it becomes less valuable when the advice comes across as directives without the corresponding experience and learnings behind it.

By following the Gestalt Protocol and using 'I' instead of 'You' when giving advice, we speak more about our experience, sharing and letting the other person understand what did and didn't work from a similar situation in the past without passing judgement on the specifics of the current scenario. When I share my personal experiences in this book with you, my hope is that you see the ups and downs of a life and not view it as a lecture or in passing judgement.

Accounting and Finance – A while ago, I was sitting down with an entrepreneur debating what to do next. It was early in the hyper growth stage of the startup and things were growing fast. Only, with limited operating history, growth expectations were even greater than reality, and there was no way the annual forecast was going to be achieved. Accountability was tied to the forecast. Their goals and metrics were tied to the forecast and so were employee bonuses.

This challenge is much more common than expected. The vast majority of entrepreneurs think they are the one in five who will be the success story. In many aspects, this startup was successful, yet fast growing startups are inherently unpredictable. Even with bottoms-up and top-down forecasts, reality is different from the spreadsheet. At some point, trying to hit a forecast that is no longer possible is more demoralizing than motivating — it is time for a reforecast.

A reforecast is simply redoing the budget and expectations after the year has already started to reflect new information. The key is to get all the stakeholders together, work to make the new forecast as accurate as possible, and then communicate it with the team. Communication is the most important part.

By over-communicating, including why the reforecast was necessary, learnings from the experience, and go-forward expectations, team members are feeling more included and more accepting of the changes. People do not expect leaders to be perfect; people expect leaders to lead and be transparent. Reforecasts are part of normal startup life. They should not happen yearly, but they do happen in the normal course of business. When a reforecast is necessary, make the changes and over-communicate with the team.

THE SLINKY® EFFECT

Harvard Business Review has an excellent article titled "What Sets Successful CEOs Apart". The authors talk about a variety of research where they distill down the four attributes that set successful CEOs apart from other CEOs. According to the article, here are the attributes: deciding with speed and conviction, engaging for impact, adapting proactively, and delivering reliably. It sounds pretty straightforward, but it is incredibly hard for a CEO to consistently do all four. Think about these characteristics as you set your calendar for the week and your intentions. By keeping these four principles in mind and in the forefront of our attention, it will frame the way we think about each situation or opportunity, improve how we feel about the job we are doing, and allow us to take the actions we can take each day to stay in alignment with these principles.

After reviewing a number of annual financial plans, both department and companywide, I have created a list of questions to ask in an attempt to help think through the high-level topics and generally make sure things make sense. A financial plan is a detailed financial model incorporating a number of elements like assumptions (e.g. ratios of account executives to sales development reps), budget line items, and specific targets (e.g. sales).

Here are eight questions to ask at an annual financial plan review:

- What are the top three takeaways from the plan? What is the big picture?
- What are the biggest risks? What are the biggest differences from the prior year's results?
- Are the ratios and assumptions in the range of other similar startups (e.g. percent of company in product development as compared to other SaaS startups)?
- Does the burn rate and the corresponding revenue growth make sense (e.g. the growth in recurring revenue should at least be larger than burn, if not a multiple of it)?

- Is the hiring plan achievable? Is there a pipeline of candidates already in place?
- What financing has to take place during the year, if any? Is there enough time to run a process?
- What product enhancements need to happen to achieve key targets like renewal rate and average revenue per account?
- What do the key metrics like revenue, revenue growth rate, gross margin, and churn rate look like? Are they trending in the right direction?

Annual financial plans are critical for startups, especially post product/market fit. Ask these eight questions and work to understand the big picture.

Operations – Excessive meetings are the blight of big companies and almost always get worse over time. Please get rid of all large meetings (more than 5 people), unless you are certain they are providing value to the whole audience. If you need a large meeting keep the meeting short (single topic announcement). Review standing meetings regularly. The review should be asking yourself if the meeting is necessary, has the meeting been effective. Otherwise, stop the recurring meeting schedule on people's calendars. Frequent meetings should be tied to an urgent project or matter. Meeting frequency should drop rapidly once the urgent matter is resolved.

Changing our perception about rudeness. We can gracefully exit - leave a meeting or end a call as soon as it is obvious you are not adding value. It is not rude to leave; it is rude to make someone stay and waste their time.

As a leader of a large firm, we have a unique language that was largely a string of acronyms or nonsense words for objects, software, or processes. It is not a good practice; it took time and energy to speak to corporate on Fridays at the office and normal business language with the clients the majority of the week. In general, anything that requires an explanation inhibits communication. We do not want people to have to memorize a glossary just to function at our company.

Communication should travel via the shortest path necessary to get the job done, not through the "chain of command". After working at over 70 client businesses in the past 20 years, I can attest that a major source of issues is poor communication between departments. The way to solve this is to allow free flow of information between all levels. If, in order to get something done between depts, an individual contributor has to talk to their manager, who talks to a director, who talks to a VP, who talks to another VP, who talks to a director, who talks to a manager, who talks to someone doing the actual work, then mistakes things will happen. It must be ok for people to talk directly and just make the right thing happen. We sometimes have trouble imaging that as leaders of a smaller scale business, yet, the habits and processes we set, if fragmented at a small scale,can become bottlenecks as you are now scaling up for the next big thing. As you evaluate what is working or not, always pick common sense as your guide. If following a "company rule" is obviously ridiculous in a particular situation, such that it would make for a great Dilbert cartoon, then the rule should change.

Customer Retention - One of the holy grails of successful SaaS businesses is having the expansion of existing customers outweigh customer churn. Meaning, if the business did not sign any new customers in a year, the upgrades for existing customers would be more money than the lost revenue from customers that leave, resulting in growth for the company. A business that does not have to sell anything new, but still grows, is in an enviable position.

Here are a few benefits when customer expansion outpaces churn:

More Money to Acquire Customers – When customers continually grow their account, more money can be spent to acquire the initial account, providing additional options for customer acquisition.

Faster Growth Rates – The law of large numbers starts to kick in making it hard to grow fast at greater scale. When customer expansion is more than churn, it makes it easier to grow faster as there is a built-in growth engine.

Raising Money – Investors look for unit economics that show the fundamentals of the business are strong and provide excellent customer expansion, along with customer renewals, and gross margins are three of the most important metrics making it easier to raise money.

One the other hand, once business begins scaling, leaders from each team start asking for more resources (e.g. we just signed 10 more customers, let us hire another person to do 'X'). Only, outside the budget, it is difficult to assess the overall efficiency. One of the best metrics to track efficiency is revenue per employee.

Over time, the revenue per employee changes as the startup scales from pre-revenue through to seed stage and beyond. Each milestone often has a higher revenue per employee with ones at the expansion stage typically having $200,000 or more in revenue per employee.

One of our operational review meeting line items should be to track our own revenue per employee and benchmark it against other startups of similar size and scale. Recently I was talking to an entrepreneur that had just finished an exercise to make his business more efficient and reduce the burn rate. After making a concerted effort over 30 days to cut waste, they now are projected to save $200,000/year. Here are a few areas to analyze:

Credit Cards – Start with the elephant in the room. We discussed the merits, process, and pitfalls of investor financing. As a result, it is common to self-fund or bootstrap our business growth. Credit cards are so easy — almost too easy — to buy stuff and we do not always scrutinize the purchases. Take last month's statement and make the cardholders justify each expense.

Amazon Web Services – Cloud platforms make it incredibly simple to scale services and scale the bill. Walk through every line item of the last AWS bill and the corresponding usage of that item (e.g. do you need all those full-time EC2 instances when spot instances might work instead? What about reserved instances?)

Unused SaaS Apps – With so many interesting SaaS apps out there it is easy to sign up and pay to not truly integrate the app into the business process such that there's little-to-no value. Go ahead and cancel it.

Unused SaaS App Users – Many SaaS apps are mission critical must-have products but that does not mean paying for more than you need. How many users of your CRM, finance software, do you have? Do you really need them all? What other apps can be consolidated?

Entrepreneurs would do well to audit expenses at least annually, if not more frequently, and cut the waste. Just because you need to move fast does not mean you need to waste money.

Accountability - it is a great time to review the end of the quarter process. In the pre product/market fit days, there is not much process to follow but as the startup grows and scales, it is important to scale the processes as well. Here are a few ideas to consider:

Simplified One Page Strategic Plan – The one pager is the overall business alignment doc. Priorities change every quarter, along with the basic metrics, but much of the document stays the same.

Quarterly Check-ins – Whether it is monthly or quarterly check-ins, it is critical to spend time with team members and constantly calibrate. With small startups, it is more ad hoc and formalizes as the business grows.

Monthly SaaS Metrics – While the one pager has great high-level info, the monthly metrics sheet breaks it down into dozens of data points and provides a fine-grained view into the performance of the business.

Start, Stop, Continue – What is working well, not working, and needs to change in the business? It is important to evaluate the overall business functions as well. Figure out what is right for the startup and continuously evolve the rhythm, data, and priorities.

Whenever I meet with an entrepreneur that is raising money, I ask about current funding, burn rate, and the number of months of runway. Managing cash and understanding the corresponding business unit economics are two critical functions of an entrepreneur, yet many do not do it. In fact, ensuring that there's always enough cash in the bank is one of the most important things a CEO does.

Every month, entrepreneurs should be able to answer these three questions immediately: How much cash do we have, how much cash are we burning each month, and how many months do we have until we run out of money?

Pretty simple, right? Only many entrepreneurs I talk to cannot answer these three questions with confidence. Entrepreneurs need to understand the importance of cash and manage it accordingly. In the software as a service, SaaS, world, gross margins are assumed to be in the 75-85% range such that the heuristics, like the golden metric for SaaS – $1 burned for $1 of recurring revenue is consistent from company to company. Yet, most companies do not have SaaS gross margins and different cost of goods sold, such that when thinking about metrics and best practices, they should be recalibrated for the gross margins of the specific company. Meaning, if the Golden Metric for SaaS is $1 of cash burned for $1 of net new annual recurring revenue, that assumes 80% gross margins. If the company has 40% gross margins, the Golden Metric would be $1 of cash burned for $2 of net new annual recurring revenue (half the margin so needs twice the revenue).

Whenever you hear metrics and best practices mentioned, factor in the gross margin. In the SaaS world, one of the common best practices is to have the cost of customer acquisition be equal to or less than the first year's revenue (or even better to be a gross margin). So, if on average it costs $5,000 in fully loaded sales and marketing expense to acquire a customer that pays $5,000 per year, things are going well. After learning that heuristic and working with a number of entrepreneurs, I've come to take it one step further and judge the success-to-date of a startup based on the amount of money burned all-time vs the annual recurring run-rate today, especially if it's one to one.

While burning $1 to get $1 of recurring revenue might not sound like much, it is actually really good. Think of a company that is growing fast at $5 million recurring on $5 million burned all-time. In today's market, that company is likely valued at $30M.- $40M (6-8x run-rate). Spending $5M to build a company worth that much is likely a good scenario for everyone involved including the founders, employees, and investors. A common phrase in the startup world is "If the company sells for 10x the amount of money raised, everyone does well". While a valuation of 10x the capital raised is excellent, consider the ratio of capital burned all-time to current recurring revenue as another metric to evaluate the success of a startup.

Product Management - A common thread I have heard over the past 20 years coming from any size and stage company was that the founder or CIO felt that if they could hire another developer and add one more important feature to their product, customers would start buying. In the book "Angel" by Jason Calacanis, he describes this as the "feature death march" where the business leader has had limited success to date and feels if they just add one more major feature, customers will start buying.

Prospects saying, they will purchase the product when it has one more feature is often an excuse. If the prospect is serious, and the feature fits the entrepreneur's vision, get the prospect to commit to buying the product now with a timeline for when the feature will be done. Ask for a signed contract. Once a contract is involved and terms are negotiated, it gets serious. Too often entrepreneurs go on a feature death march only to bring the new feature back to the prospect and have them still say "no" and ask for another, different feature or outright say they will not buy it.

Missing an important feature can be a legitimate reason for a prospect to say "no" but more often than not, it is an excuse and they will never buy. Figure out the difference and do not go on a blind feature death march.

FreshBooks created a separate company, with a separate team, in a separate office, to build a new competitor called BillSpring. BillSpring's goal was to build a real business with its own customer base, that if successful, would replace the original FreshBooks product. After two years, BillSpring was working well and customers loved it. FreshBooks made the BillSpring product the new FreshBooks product while maintaining the legacy product and not forcing customers to switch. Now, FreshBooks has a platform for the future. If you need to reinvent your company, consider building a competing company, internally.

Recently I was talking to an entrepreneur that is in the process of changing their data storage architecture as the startup is growing fast and there are increased demands on the database. Only, the app is performing fine and there are not any slowdowns right now, but it is clear that with the continued growth at some point there will be issues. Yet, the team does not know exactly when that will occur, even after some load and stress tests against the system. Now, they are moving forward with a heavy refactoring of code and changing of the storage architecture.

Balancing the short-term and long-term product demands is never easy. Here are a few questions to ask:

- What percentage of current customers will appreciate this change? What percentage of desired customers will appreciate this change?
- Do we have to implement this change eventually? Why? Why not? What instrumentation will help guide our decision-making process?
- What does the current road map have prioritized? What will have to change to make room to implement this long-term product change now?
- Is the proposed change a temporary solution or will it support growth indefinitely?
- What are the risks? What might go wrong?
- How will this change affect our ability to compete in the market?

Balancing short-term and long-term product demands is never easy. Ask these questions and make an informed decision.

Contracts - As an investor, I like seeing portfolio companies have their customers sign annual (or multi-year) contracts and get the benefit of cash flow predictability (including prepayment) and customer commitment. In exchange for doing a longer customer contract, the vendor company can invest more in the customer acquisition process, the onboarding/implementation process, and on-going customer success and support.

As a buyer, I dislike contracts as the needs of the business can change (need to cancel or downgrade — not possible), the vendor can provide poor service or a poor product experience for a period of time and there's no recourse, and product usage can fluctuate (Slack is famous for only charging for users that actually use the product, not all users in the system). No contracts and more flexibility to adjust spending (specifically spending less during certain months) is more customer centric.

Over time, as more next generation SaaS companies emerge, and there's more comparable competition in the market, I believe we're going to see that more SMB software vendors not require contracts and have more flexible business practices that better align with how users want to buy. This will be a slow transition but expect it to be mainstream in the next 5 – 10 years.

Sales and Marketing - Early on, it is critical to understand the customer's problem. Too often, we come up with an idea that is good for us but falls flat with the potential customer. Use the customer discovery method to understand the problem without trying to sell them on the existing idea. Here are a few things to keep in mind with customer discovery interviews:

These can be done in focus groups or individually. Some key principles apply to really get constructive feedback. Think through how the interview questions are worded and try to uncover an inherent bias in the wording that can distort your results. Use the same scale and consistent wording so the math lines up correctly. Establish a clear zero to five scale with the wording of a question always having the low value equal low satisfaction. It is all too common to try and guide the potential customer down a path that is consistent with our existing idea. The point is not validation, it is honest opinion.

Ask broad, open-ended questions, and remember the old adage: humans have two ears and one mouth for a reason — you listen twice as much as you talk. After listening, ask follow-up questions that build your understanding of how things work currently with as much minute detail as you can uncover. Find out what the ideal solution would be if time and money were not an issue, if you could wave a magic wand and have anything you wanted, what would it be?

Never show any prototypes you might have until after you have asked all your main questions. Again, do not introduce bias. We would do well to use customer discovery to deeply understand the customer's problem and work to ignore their existing ideas.

As the cost to build an app has gone down over the last 10 years due to open source and cloud computing, the number of apps as grown. Now, there are dozens of apps that do the same thing in every category imaginable. The result: customer acquisition is the number one challenge with so much noise in the market. And, it is only going to get more challenging.

Here are four elements in a customer acquisition repeatable process: first build a community. – Work towards 1,000 true fans. Start small. Find the first 10 that care. Then the first 100. Nurture the community and grow it over time. Write original content or work with a marketing person who coaches you to improve. Be authentic but, make a statement, tell the story of why this product, now. Keep the conversation going, put new ideas out there. Find a rhythm. Engage with your community, show up where they show up to connect with people. Monitor your sales and marketing efforts to validate and target our best fit accounts. Run a process that shows who your most valuable customers are, not the one-off customers. Follow the account-based engagement best practices. Constantly experiment, change one variable at a time so you know if it is working or not. Try new ideas like micro apps and social selling.

Customer acquisition is the most difficult challenge required for startups to succeed. Invest in it early and build the expertise over time.

If you are still a business leader and considering becoming an entrepreneur, starting a blog to share some of your thoughts with the universe is a good search option. See what resonates and what falls flat before you even start down the road. After hemming and hawing, he said he just likes to consume content. True, consuming content is fun and easy, but it does not force thinking through ideas and articulating a position. The act of producing content, even for an audience of one, while difficult at first, gets easier with time.

Another entrepreneur I met with recently was asking for go to market ideas for her new product. With a focus on small businesses, it was clear that the cost of customer acquisition would have to be low based on the product price point, and that it was going to require a light-to-no touch sales process. I asked about search engine optimization (SEO) and content marketing only to have her lament that they had tried it without much luck. SEO and content marketing, just like most endeavors, takes a significant amount of time and energy to be successful. The best time to start producing content was years ago. The next best time to start is now.

Spend time producing content, not just consuming it. Whether it is simple tweets on Twitter, or long-form articles, entrepreneurs would do well to start writing more frequently. Take the time, put in the effort, develop the muscle — it is not easy, but, ultimately, it is worth it. Most startups struggle with sales — often in conjunction with not having product/market fit— making for a high likelihood of failure. Here are four ideas proven tips for finding customers: Partner with the first three beta accounts and charge them whatever they're willing to pay so that they'll be references and provide testimonials, investing in them, so their success helps you understand your next round of customers and gives valuable feedback on your product. Spend time with investors and use their connections to find potential prospects, form a customer advisory board and use it as a way to entice potential customers, and deliver a good mix of targeted social, email, and event marketing alongside clear messaging to help your voice be heard.

Big companies make sales and marketing look easy, since they have had years to develop and improve their processes. Be genuine and authentic and do it, iterate, learn, and do better.

Account Management - quantifying account-based engagement efforts for your sales team, even if that sales team is us. Let us say you have accounts rated by tier with the 'A' accounts being best fits, the 'B' accounts being the second tier, the 'C' accounts being the third tier, and so on. How do you decide how much effort to devote to each tier?

There are two common approaches:

Minutes-Based - Take the most common activities such as a phone call, initial email, email reply, and demo and allocate a number of minutes for each as a target for effort. For example, you might start with five minutes for an email, 20 minutes for an email reply, and 90 minutes for a demo including prep work. Then, figure out the ideal mix of activities and the corresponding minutes per sales rep per week, assuming 40 hours: a sample might look like 5 hours – general meetings, coaching, 25 hours – 50 Tier 1 accounts at 30 minutes each, 10 hours – 40 Tier 2 accounts at 15 minutes each, Total: 90 accounts engaged

Build a CRM report by activity type with a formula to multiply by the number of minutes allocated and then group by the account tier to see the results.

Touches-Based - Here again you take the most common touches (call, email, social media interaction, InMail message) and assume each is roughly the same amount of effort. Take the number of Tier 1 accounts and Tier 2 accounts and start with 2x the effort for Tier 1 accounts. Assign a required number of touches per Tier 1 account and per Tier 2 account each week.

Build a CRM report by activity type grouped by the account tier to ensure the efforts match the required number of touches. Quantifying account-based engagement efforts takes work to set up and requires an on-going process. Every sales leader knows that more effort equals more results, and this strategy is excellent for more predictable revenue.

Strategy - One of the reasons so few entrepreneurs spend time on a strategic plan is the belief that it is time consuming and difficult. From my experience, the simpler, more concise, the better. Here is a simple guide for a basic strategic plan:

- What do you do? Why?
- Who do you serve? Why?
- What are the measurable goals? Current values? Target values?
- What are the priorities? Who owns them?

We want to build an enduring business. A business that provides value to all stakeholders, grows in perpetuity, and has the ability to generate sustainable profits is the true measure of success. Should a strategic buyer come along, great. If not, no worries.

In fact, in today's market, if a startup is venture backed, we are required to be on a path to $100M+ in revenue to have the opportunity to go public. Going public is an "exit" in that shareholders get liquidity and the company raises money from the public markets (assuming it is not a direct listing). Going public is the exit venture backed startups should focus on.

If a potential investor asks about an exit strategy, the answer should be to build a large, enduring business. Then, and only if the investor is looking for more specifics, we offer up the logical acquirers for the business. Too many investors ask about an exit strategy, when, in reality, the world does not work that way. Companies are bought, not sold.

Build a great business and acquirers will come knocking; everything else is conjecture.

The strategic plan is not a onetime activity. I believe, even with limited people and resources, a strategic plan is worthwhile. As a tool to communicate with employees, advisors, mentors, and investors, it is invaluable. When meeting with entrepreneurs I like to ask to see their strategic plan. Many times, I require seeing a simple strategic plan as a prerequisite before meeting so as to have a more informed conversation. Only, the vast majority of the time, no strategic plan exists, simple or otherwise. Then, when a strategic plan is present, and we go through several of the items, it becomes clear that it is out-of-date and/or not remotely achievable. What gives? One of the reasons so few entrepreneurs spend time on a strategic plan is the belief that it is time consuming and difficult. From my experience, the simpler, more concise, the better.

More complicated strategic plans are less likely to be updated and maintained, rendering them nearly useless. Finding a balance that has enough value but is not cumbersome is key. We build, regularly update, and share their strategic plans. Keep it simple. Keep it accurate. Keep it worthwhile.

Technology is More than Your Product – it is easy for technology entrepreneurs as business leaders to focus on the technology of their product offering more than the technology that services our operations. We begin with simple applications that allow easy access and serve a particular function for the business. As we scale our business, we need to remain curious about the options before us as we live in a technology boom, where technology companies have surpassed in pervasiveness and earning the previous mainstays from manufacturing and industry.

Leveraging SaaS Applications - In SaaS 2.0, the product is the sales and marketing. Everything starts and ends with the product so there are no barriers to begin using the app immediately. Once signed into the free edition of the app (often called the platform), there are marketing videos that explain the benefits of each module. Paid modules are explained and in-app upgrades made clear — the selling is done by the app, in the app. Sales reps are still available, but they're there as consultants to answer questions and help with change management, not to get contracts signed. There are no contracts to sign.

The most powerful form of service is high quality self-service with great people to help as a backup. With SaaS 2.0, the product is the sales and marketing. I believe we will see more apps incorporate free trials and other mechanisms to experience the app before buying. As mentioned before, it continues with the consumerization of IT where people want their business apps to feel like their consumer apps and trying something out is no different.

When we leverage SaaS applications to run our business, it reduces overhead of having an in-house IT department to analyze business requirements, build, test, and maintain the applications. However, as we scale up, we may need to scale to large SaaS applications to avoid having our technology become our bottleneck for customer attraction, retention, and operational backbone for Finance, HR, supply chain, etc. The activities associated with the applications are addressed in the operations section above, as a result.

The flip side of this is one of the biggest challenges for startups is the lack of third-party integrations. One of the strongest network effects for SaaS platforms happens when hundreds of other products build integrations to connect data and processes. Think for example about Atlanta's MailChimp. The more integrations a customer uses, the harder it is to switch vendors.

As expected, there are SaaS products that specialize in integrating other SaaS and installed products:

MuleSoft– Enterprise strength integration platform that is heavily customizable.

Zapier– Huge breadth of integrations in a do-it-yourself fashion. This should be the starting point for most people looking to connect apps.

Cloud Elements– The Cloud integration approach permits a single hub for multiple connections. This connectivity is a huge timesaver for more sophisticated custom integrations. Look for cloud integration middleware to be a key part of the solution for next generation SaaS apps. However, keep in mind that security requirements are enhanced with this approach.

The above companies are some of many that we can research for providing integration as we grow and scale. The point is not to recommend any of these because it varies by business, industry, and applications we use. For me, the point is to do your research. We have identified, as noted earlier, application development costs have dropped and there are a plethora of similar products that have their target audience, find out who their audience is and if it matches your business; not all product integrations are created equal — not even close. For SaaS 2.0 startups, catching up to the depth and variety of integrations of the incumbents is one of the major challenges. When thinking through integrations, it is important to understand the three major types:

Native Integrations – Integrations that are developed in-house to send/receive data as well as call remote functions and expose additional internal functionality are native integrations. Native integrations are the most valuable as the quality is typically higher and the SaaS company is committed to maintain them.

JavaScript Overlay Integrations – Integrations that are done via a Google Chrome Extension or JavaScript to override the user interface of a third-party app are UI overlay integrations. A common example is the industry of Chrome Extensions that add functionality to Gmail through the user interface and not the API.

Middleware Integrations – Integrations that are written and maintained by a third-party integration platform to connect two disparate apps are middleware integrations. Middleware integrations can be more expensive and/or slower depending on the APIs of the products being connected.

Tech entrepreneurs need to understand the benefits of microservices and start planning them once they hit the growth stage, but not before.

THE SLINKY® EFFECT

All major platforms going forward are going to have some form of microservices underpinning them.

Recently I was talking to an entrepreneur about APIs (ways for apps to communicate with other apps automatically) as he was looking for a way to connect his app, and corresponding customers, with a number of other apps. Only, he could not find anything on the market. Successful startups have numerous integrations but require going through their respective apps to make the connectors work — you cannot readily white label them or use their APIs to connect to other APIs. Why hasn't a universal API middleware emerged? Here are a few ideas:

APIs constantly change. Facebook was notorious about constantly breaking their API, yet their motto at the time ("move fast and break things") made their priority clear. As a vendor connecting to another vendor's API, it takes on-going resources and money to keep APIs working, which is more expensive than it looks.

APIs are not as strategic as expected for most cloud-based apps. While companies like Salesforce have a variety of APIs, many cloud-based apps do not prioritize their APIs and thus the API does not have parity with the user interface and bugs do not get fixed quickly.

The long tail is really long. While there are 25-50 apps in the mainstream category (> $100MM ARR), there are hundreds and hundreds more in the near-mainstream category (> $25MM ARR), not counting the thousands more that have at least some scale (> $10M ARR). Outside of the mainstream apps, the next tier of apps, while having a large number of customers, does not have enough overlapping customers with any other non-mainstream apps, making for a limiting number of useful integrations.

APIs constantly have problems. Whether it is an API going down, user authentication expiring, or invalid data with limited error codes, APIs constantly have challenges. This makes for a less-than-ideal end user experience and a challenge to support a large number of APIs at scale.

Bottom line: APIs are much more complicated than they seem and only a handful are needed to make most customers happy, so vendors just write their own hand-crafted integrations. It does not fulfill the ideals of a universal API middleware platform, but it is good enough for most apps.

CRM and Marketing Machine Learning Apps - When thinking through the integration landscape, it is important to understand that there are a variety of integration types and they are not equal.

Considering marketing automation platforms collect so much information about leads through email opens, form submissions, web page visits, e-book downloads, webinar signups, etc., there is a tremendous amount of training data for machine learning to find insights.

Marketing automation is essentially human-defined rules based on what they think is best (e.g. send email A, wait two days, send email B, etc.) Machine learning "learns" over time and can figure out patterns humans cannot because there are too many dimensions to analyze. Here are a few ideas on how to use machine learning in marketing automation:

Email Send Time– Analyze when leads opened emails in the past and automatically schedule future emails to be sent at the same time (time of day, day of week, etc.)

Email Message to Trigger– Analyze what emails (or other types of content) were most closely associated with pushing the lead through the current phase of the lifecycle (e.g. engaging with a sales rep) and trigger the email automatically (as opposed to human-defined static rules).

Lead to Opportunity Probability– Analyze every piece of historical data for leads that turned into opportunities (the training data or learning set) and come up with a probability for the remainder of the leads.

Lead to Customer Probability– Like the lead to opportunity probability, do the same thing for leads that became customers (not just those that had an opportunity in the pipeline associated with them) and come up with a probability that any given lead will become a customer.

Machine learning has applications in all fields, especially marketing automation. Look for existing vendors to add this type of functionality as well as new vendors to emerge to take advantage of this new technology.

Predictive Analytics – Artificial Intelligence - One of the sales and marketing technologies we are seeing more of is the whole predictive arena. At a simple level, applied to marketing, predictive takes existing contacts and opportunities and scores them against a dynamic model based on other contacts and opportunities that became customers. Put another way: find great-fit companies that look like our existing customers so we can target them.

Account-based sales and marketing platforms solve the major problem of running programs in a scalable manner against hundreds (or thousands) of target accounts. Traditional marketing and sales as the opportunity progresses through the funnel, casts a net, sees what is caught, and then works the qualified leads. Now, as a more modern approach, account-based sales and marketing goes spear fishing and proactively seeks out best-fit accounts based on a number of dimensions. Only, there is often not an easy way to find and refine best-fit accounts — enter predictive technologies.

Here are a few thoughts on predictive sales and marketing technologies. Your competition will be employing these technologies. Artificial Intelligence and machine learning are key components of websites, customer relationship management systems, computers, appliances, cars, phones, office buildings, trucks, manufacturing plants, warehouses, etc. This data is used to predict buying behaviors and customer demand to help companies build on demand, ship on demand, and deliver on demand to reduce overhead for materials, storage, workforce, and a variety of other costs. The ability to get the most of these systems is not to just merely have them, but to have the deep understanding of the value chain. Predicting customer behavior that is generic, is merely information, but predicting customer information based on their values is wisdom that can be acted on and set you apart. Combing through billions of records by hand is simply not possible for most small businesses.

Look for the category of predictive sales and marketing systems to grow fast as the technology crosses the chasm and becomes more well-known.

The larger the product, the harder it is to make changes to it due to all the dependencies. Amazon was the first major technology company to realize that Internet scale, and its greater levels of complexity, requires a new way of building large-scale systems: microservices. Microservices are simply smaller, self-sufficient special purpose products that form a platform (e.g. tiny apps that are used to make a big app). Amazon went further and built Amazon Web Services (AWS) to make the backend of these microservices even easier to manage and scale, and now AWS is one of the fastest products to $10 billion in annual revenue ever.

Blockchain - The early internet dealt with intangibles. We sent or received emails, corresponded on forums, and read and distributed articles. This modern internet deals with assets, or our most valuable immediate items that we can touch and want to protect. These assets are stored in encoded form on a network-to-network chain called the blockchain or ledger, where each participant sees who we do business with. This not only protects our business dealings and prevents theft, but, also, simplifies our affairs, quickens the process, reduces errors, and saves us from hiring a third party.

This decentralized blockchain system is going to change our lives from the way you transact business or manage assets, to the way you use your machines, vote, rent a car, and even prove who we are. Along the way, it will transform banks and other financial institutions, hospitals, companies, and governments, among others. The security of blockchain is the enabler behind this technology. The code is distributed across the ledger, rather than stored in tables in earlier generation applications and systems.

Simply put, more people than ever before have super computers in their pocket with tremendous functionality and ease of use. Incredibly large markets with new functionality result in huge opportunities, and we have a tech boom as a result.

Discernment Combined with Curiosity

At this juncture, we have discussed many topics that are broad ranging around starting or running a successful business. With curiosity we also need discernment. There are so many options and so many tasks, it is easy to see why we overlook or discard the importance of some of the contents of the book. It is about alignment, build your strategy around your vision, and take all subsequent activities in that same alignment. Along with alignment it is about scale. Many of the tasks outlined herein take under an hour per week. We can think back to the tools we use, the apps and calendar to prioritize our calendar each day, week, month, and quarter to make time to complete all of our critical tasks. Then we use the Continue, Delegate, and Stop method to determine when to hire a virtual assistant, full time assistant, or other staff as our business scales.

Evoke Respect

We know the saying that respect is earned. We have built our business for social impact and the underlying assumption within the book is that we are operating with honesty, integrity, and what is good and right for all. When we heed our calling by universal intelligence, we can validate our vision by staying true to these five basic tenants.

1. Notice what you are noticing – see the reaction and count to 10. The ability to stop and respond vs. reacting is unique to humans and generally produces better outcomes.

2. Identifying your longing and discontent – This awareness points you to the weakest link in your value chain and underscores where you can allow discomfort in an area that is going well, for a defined period of time, in the interest of improving the weaker area

3. Define what we would love. Having a burning desire and passion for what we do is our personal guidepost to get us through the ups and downs of life? For it to be a vision, not a goal, it must be bigger than you. You will need faith, mindset, and a team. You may not know all the steps; life is not that clear cut. The next key is knowing and believing that your vision is in alignment with your core values. When we act with authenticity and genuine joy for what we are embarking on, we do not second guess the decision. When we are in spiritual and internal alignment, we act with civility to everyone and are transparent in our vision and our capabilities and remain curious to see who comes into our orbit to connect with and grow our business and full spectrum life vision.

4. Unedited Sourcing of the next steps - editing disrupts the natural flow of ideas, so just put all the ideas down on paper, record them on your phone, whatever works for you. Keep it going for a minimum of 30 minutes as the first 10-20 minutes are often older ideas that have not made their way to paper or other media yet, then the new ideas start flowing if you let them. Then, you can see what resonates and prioritize the remaining ideas then set a date to accomplish them.

5. Take Action – even the turtle crosses the finish line. Do not let fear, doubt, or worry derail you. I saw a great meme the other day. Giving up after failure is like slashing the other three tires when you get a flat tire. Yes, something bad may happen along the way, but who knows the flat tire may have kept you from being involved in a fatal accident a few miles up the road. Stay

on course until number 3 does not apply anymore, then change course at the next intersection.

We earn respect when we remain centered on not own our link in the value chain, but the entire value chain and how it works together for the benefit of all.

Evoke Resiliency

There are many types of business leaders. Many are executives for a corporation in a middle to upper management role. Their focus is often on the performance of their division or department and how their area drives value for the corporation's shareholders. Others are Chief Executive Officers (CEOs). While the scale of their organization varies, their objective is to see that the organization structure as a whole, meets its vision, mission, and objectives, and reports to a Board of Directors.

Still others are self-employed. They formed a company, frequently based on their particular technical expertise (accountant, tax, lawyer, doctor, hairstylist, baker, carpenter, electrician, plumber, etc.). They instinctively understand there is a demand for these talents and prefer to work on their own rather than for an organization, no matter what size the organization is.

We find ourselves, as business leaders, in a variety of different situations. For some, we are embarking on a new challenge, initiative, or launching a business. Others choose to work in a business that is on a steady state path and we navigate through ambiguity. Some are facing a new or persistent threat to the viability of their business.

Resiliency is a characteristic that transcends the labels, circumstances, and situations by adhering to a common principle. If we direct our focus on defining our business around our value, then we take the actions required to remain relevant. We explore a variety of leadership types, stages of a business lifecycle, and real life examples in how we can apply them in defining our businesses around this value chain: our values as a potential business owner, our clients' needs, the needs of our investors and if you are a social business, our cause.

There was a lot of buzz around exponential leadership in 2019. Digital Transformation is changing the future of work, how companies are organized, and their portfolio of products and services at an ever-increasing pace. This was a foreshadowing of the accelerated pace of change that was initiated by government response at a global, national, and local level during the 2020 COVID pandemic. The opportunities revealed at this time propelled some businesses to heightened success and the lack of response revealed the underlying weakness of other businesses and sent them spiraling in the opposite direction.

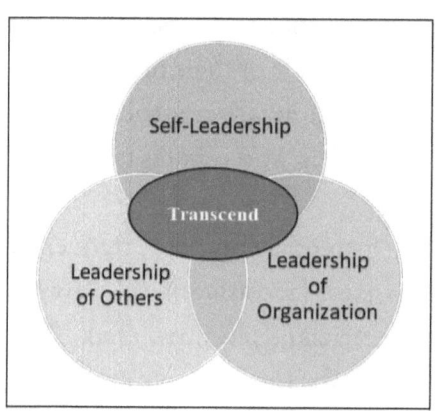

Yet, the principles of agility and iterative development are rooted in the American Renaissance founded in Concord, Massachusetts in 1830s led by Ralph Waldo Emerson and Henry David Thoreau. It is a social movement and idealistic philosophy in which knowledge about us and the world around us "transcends" what we can see, hear, taste, touch, or feel.

Beginning in 1836, Emerson hosted a series of Transcendental Club Mastermind meetings at his home. The goal was to apply the concept of a unique DNA, or our unique gift for being born into this world and how to break free from an educational, church, and society that valued normalization. They shared their individual perspectives on how to live productive lives while walking their own unique path, not the path designed by convention, rules, and traditional thinking. These same principles are applicable today as we continue to delve into Generative Artificial Intelligence and design businesses that reap the benefits, while holding true to our moral and ethical center.

New always has the following effect – anxiety over the unknown. Left unchecked anxiety grows into being scared, scared grows into fear, and fear can lead to paranoia and blocks in moving forward. Redirected to a new perspective, we can generate excitement around the possibilities. As humans we are complex beings and can hold multiple emotions, opinions, and assimilate facts. We frequently get stuck when these lead to conflicting signals or we do not recognize the warning signs of escalation of anxiety.

Dynamic situations lead to both opportunity and ambiguity. Generative AI relies on the interaction of the human and computer intelligence. AI is amazing at chunking through vast data stores and making associations. However, humans excel at causality intelligence. An association of two components gets at an indistinct correlation of the two, yet without human intelligence, it does not know if the relationship is cause and effect. AI can predict an upcoming failure of a machine, based on the sensory readings, but it cannot understand what conditions are causing the abnormal sensors. It takes a person who understands how the software was developed along with someone who knows the business to detect if the failure can be prevented by maintenance, was caused by a minor mishap and can be prevented or if the failure is unavoidable. It is also important to understand the process to order the replacement parts and schedule the repair prior to not only the failure, but the ripple effects.

This partnership between AI and the business leader relies on the partnership between a technology that can sort through mass amounts of data to sort, analyze, and retrieve the correlations, and the business leader who applies their six mental faculties of imagination, intuition, perception, memory, reason, and will to identify the underlying forces of the world, that the programmer didn't include in their code.

To live a fully dimensional life in a modern nuanced society, this book goes beyond the traditional vision, strategy, and tactics by understanding that the essence of who we define ourselves to be and the resulting patterns of behavior we have adopted to get to this point create the awareness and aliveness in our vision that is our Why.

Evoke Flexibility

Some people confuse flexibility with being malleable. This is not my intent. The Slinky® is made of metal yet is flexible and retains its structure. This is the aspect of flexibility that we want to adopt or retain. I enjoy this particular definition of a leader and leadership:

Leader - Anyone who causes movement to occur.

Leadership- co-creating coordinated movement, causing the actions necessary to produce the desired result.

In each chapter, we have seen how the metaphors of leadership played out in all dimensions of the pyramid above. Our foundation is understanding our innate guidance, regardless of your religious orientation. This then forms patterns of behavior that have served us up until we read this book. Then we have the ability to create a richly textured vision that goes beyond a single sentence we see in businesses today to look at all dimensions of our life to see the intersections and integrations. Then, you apply the right strategy and tactics to move you from just thinking about your vision to architecting change.

Let us explore a common quote from Henry David Thoreau:

> "I learned this, at least, by my experiment: that if one advances confidently in the direction of his dreams, and endeavors to live the life which he has imagined, he will meet with a success unexpected in common hours."

We often see this quote shortened to end here. Yet the key to the quote is to continue on through the next sentence.

> "He will put some things behind, will pass an invisible boundary; new, universal, and more liberal laws will begin to establish themselves around and within him; or the old laws be expanded, and interpreted in his favor in a more liberal sense, and he will live with the license of a higher order of beings."

There is a point of sufficiency (invisible boundary), where, if we stop before reaching it, we do not see the results. Yet, after reaching that point, we need to be aware of the new "operating system" we have installed and notice the changing dynamics and respond accordingly to reach the point where we live our vision that has been created.

Here is an easy, fun example of how leadership matters in how our message is delivered and can produce wildly different outcomes, when we empower ourselves, others, and our organization.

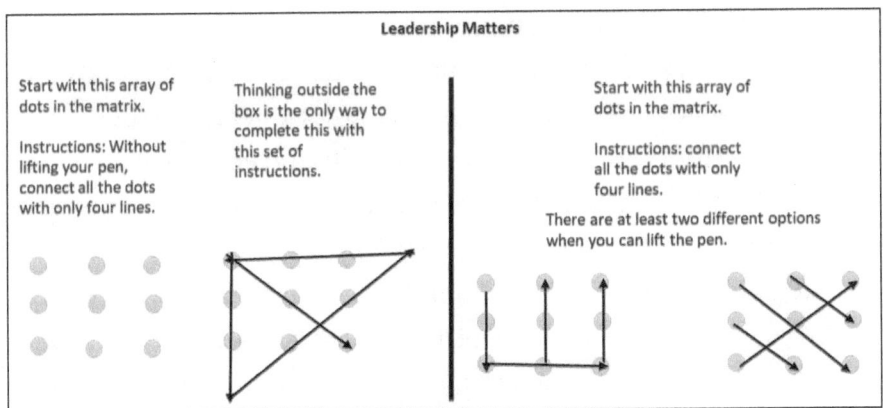

You will see that a slight difference in the directions, without lifting your pen, versus omitting those words, leads to a completely different outcome. If your goal is creativity, there is minimal impact, yet, if you are conveying a vision from the CEO, you may end up wildly off the mark. As business leaders we will do well to keep this quote from R.D. Laing in mind.

> "The range of what we think and do is limited by what we fail to notice. It is because we fail to notice, there is little we can do to change. until we notice how failing to notice shapes our thoughts and deeds".

Noticing our lives, rather than stepping through the patterns of our life is the essence of exponential and dynamic leadership. This core competency serves as a foundation when our businesses experience disruption from the digital age, a health emergency, or other situations where resiliency and curiosity are lynchpins in charting and navigating a path starting in ambiguity and finding opportunity.

Evoke Abundance

During the pandemic, there were heartbreaking stories of people who moved from abundance to the brink of homelessness. How did that happen? Did they not reinvest profits of their business into building a foundation that can be shaken and not crumble? In California and other countries around the Pacific Rim, people, governments, and businesses have learned from past earthquakes and implemented stronger building codes and reinforcements that provide the basis for standing firm in turbulent times. When we create a MS Word document, we have the latitude to change the margins from the standard defaults to different smaller margins. When we adopt those changes, we need to look at the print view of the document to see if meaningful content will be cutoff. The same concept works for evoking abundance. We start with a mindset of success, but also in not taking risks that undercut our success just outside of our current focus.

Abundance applies not only to our bottom line. It is the wealth that comes from creating a workplace where people enjoy the work, the interaction, and feel valued in their contributions. It is choosing how to fill your calendar with activities that build your business, build your family ties, and generate the free time to pursue other areas of interest and invest in our health.

CHAPTER NINE

EXPLORE

> **Your story of an enduring, vibrant sustainable business**

This book is about the joy that the Slinky® toy and others inspired as I explored possibilities as a child and continue to explore as I continue to retain my curiosity as an adult. If we retain that fundamental curiosity we come to understand that the more we know the more there is to learn. We don't see the differences between the titles of business leaders and entrepreneurs as semantics. We see both perspectives of the difference between being self-employed and creating a thriving business. Yet, we likely also saw that like with all humanity there are many similarities that bind us as business leaders as well.

The goal of investing in yourself to bring out the imagination to solve your customer's problem requires the ability to flip our perspective from what brings us value to what brings value to others. Each day we face the ups and downs of the challenges of a life cycle of a business where we leverage another set of capabilities in applying our intuition and reason in making critical business decisions on a wide range of topics. These topics cover every aspect of the business and the business relationships we make to develop an ecosystem of support. We call upon our sense of will do the thing that will propel us forward, even when every cell in our brain is saying no, this is too hard.

What is the essence that we hold that provides the center that this all emanates from? It is our tie to our "Why". Some call it our purpose, our vision, mission, or other synonyms. We sometimes struggle to articulate it well, because it is so deep within us, we can allow it to become buried with the day-to-day activities. Yet, if we get in alignment with it, it is the source of our power. It allows us to decide to be happy in the midst of the chaos when it is coming together. It is the guiding light that pulls us back on course when we lose sight of the path or face a fork in the road. It adds fun and joy to the journey by pulling us to look at all aspects of our life and construct a business that doesn't overwhelm us with long hours, drudgery, and the resulting tradeoff in losing time with the relationships we value so much that are driving us to do the work we do in the world.

My approach is to look at our lives as business leaders from a holistic perspective. We can have it all, maybe not in every given day, but we can construct a business and life that ebb and flow with the changes we experience. How is this done? By knowing enough of the science behind the theory to trust that it works and not trust in the false messaging of instant gratification. This is the fundamental essence of sustainability. We plant seeds today for each of the four dimensions of our lives. Some seeds are annuals and they grow quickly, come to maturity, and are harvested. Others are like hardwood trees and bamboo. They set a strong root system first. They penetrate into the various layers of soil to find sources of water and nutrients that are not obvious and easy. This gives them the power and energy to sustain them in times of periodic drought and other conditions that come their way.

This concept is not unique to nature, we can build it into our businesses intentionally. Let us look at the automobile industry for a variety of examples of how enduring can show up. I am a huge fan of classic automobiles and Chasing Classic Cars is one of my favorite TV shows. One of the things I enjoy most about living in the southeast US is the preponderance of classic car meetup shows. The variety of cars and restoration approaches (restoration, modernization, customization, and hot rods) fascinates me. While I love looking at the cars, I also love hearing the stories and seeing the scrapbooks the owners bring to chronicle the difference in condition between when they acquired the car and today. The love and work they poured into the effort have created joy not only in creating something beautiful, but in the lifestyle, they have adopted by going to these shows and meeting and engaging with people like me.

The picture is from a recent trip to California, where I went to Monterrey for the Concurs de Elegance for the auctions downtown and on the next day, I saw a variety of owners taking their cars on the drive to Big Sur.

Henry Ford took another path entirely to sustainability and building an enduring business. He never invented a car. He invented a process that took cars from a luxury item only owned by a few select wealthy people and brought it to each of the rest of us. The Model T is interesting in a variety of ways. One, we can tell from the name that his first attempt was not successful and one of the keys to building a sustainable business that endured beyond his lifetime was in building in resilience. The next thing we see is a change from the size, scale, and ornamentation down to a barebones approach to transportation. He concentrated on function over style to create a process, famously stating that you can have any color you want expect black. Yet, even Henry Ford had to listen to customer demand as other competitors hit the marketplace and found ways to satisfy the customer desire for form along with function. Not every Ford model was successful and when I was first starting to drive, the FORD acronym had become synonymous with Found On Road Dead. Whole books have been written and business textbooks are filled with case studies on the rise and fall of the Ford Motor Co. lifecycle.

Yet the main takeaway is that they have sustained their position over time, despite tremendous setbacks, even when they were self-inflicted. This happened not only because of resilience, but because Henry Ford created an amazing system of support and an ecosystem of relationships that propelled other businesses to the same level of success. Henry Firestone was one of his Mastermind group members. He also sought out Thomas Edison as his mentor. Edison's belief in Ford helped him overcome the fear, doubt, and worry associated with businesses in their formation stage. Most recently, Ford leveraged their automation and manufacturing processes to switch from automobiles to manufacturing ventilators. This is the level of agility that many small business owners do not cultivate.

The key is the alignment between what your customers desire and what you produce. While the concept is simple, it is not necessarily easy to implement. When we fall into patterns for being busy, taking back-to-back calls, and consumed by the routine of running a business, we can lose the opportunity of developing solid connections with the customers and getting authentic feedback, not just high level survey data.

Let us look at how two entrepreneurs followed different paths to creating successful businesses and lives they love, while also making an impact on their communities. Both of these entrepreneurs applied these concepts often through intuition rather than a study of human mindset and behavior, when defining their path to success. Life is about contrast and the two examples are a way of demonstrating our unique ability to chart our own journey based on our values and life experience.

Recap of an entrepreneurial journey

Emerge highlights

We are in a constant state of becoming if we are taking actions that challenge us to build on our success and look for new customers, new investors, and ways to give back to our cause. Each day does not have to be like the compressed Slinky®, it can be like the active toy in the eyes of a child who see the possibilities.

Entrepreneur A was not all about study and formal education, he was a classic Innovator. Out of high school he founded a startup that was an early retailer in the mobile communications industry that was just gaining prominence. After four years he opted for an executive sales position at a firm that specialized in enabling cashless transactions. Then back to start up again, guiding entrepreneurs in the fulfillment of corporate strategy and estate planning for high net worth individuals. As a serial entrepreneur he had gained enough experience in the emerge stage of the journey to position himself for bigger things to come. However, his original business did not reach the point of maturity to be able to sell and profit from the original business by following instincts as opposed to a proven process.

Entrepreneur B followed a more traditional path to entrepreneurship by setting an intentional strategy to complete his undergraduate and graduate degrees and worked in management development positions. Then he brought his combination of education and experience together and founded Sapient Health Network, which he co-founded and led prior to selling the firm to WebMD. He employed the value creation model as he positioned his startup for a growth to sale strategy. He generated wealth for the co-founders, acquiring entity, and the venture continues to serve the self-service health information access needs of its customers.

Extend highlights

We have seen how we can extend our influence and our business model, so we do not overreach beyond the fundamental structure required to support it. We see how a great idea can be supported by the right operational processes that deliver repeatable quality and yet still allow for customer feedback to be incorporated into what products and services we offer.

Entrepreneur A employed an effective strategy by moving from entrepreneur to executive level employee by working in a firm that specialized in working with high net worth individuals. The success he built in developing the customer knowledge and relationships helped him to extend his influence, serve needs, and gain an understanding of the premise of value creation from the lens of his customer base.

Entrepreneur B extended his influence by building a strong foundation for his business that attracted the right business to acquire his startup and then built the wealth to extend influence by giving back to local entrepreneur support for startup guidance, advisory roles on the boards of small businesses, and then a formal education role at a local university as an adjunct professor.

Expand highlights

We reviewed how our mindset, when open, can accept or reject an expansion idea based on the merits of the idea, not as a reaction to not taking a risk, that could improve our business, lead to happier customers, and drive value at each link in the value chain.

Entrepreneur A as a classic Innovator was able to parlay the influence and wealth attained from the executive position into acquiring a firm that had a strong reputation but was at an inflection point in their life cycle as their products had not been refreshed and was not attracting sufficient new business to thrive. Under his leadership over the past nearly two decades the refreshed guidance he provided helped them to expand and grow their footprint.

Entrepreneur B has taken a different path, not concentrating on the growth of his own business platform as much as focusing on small businesses in general to invest, advise, and prepare business owners to apply the principles in the value chain process to help this important sector of the local economy to thrive.

Energize highlights

After the pandemic, as restaurants were required to reopen at reduced capacity, at least one owner energized the feel of her restaurant by bringing in a variety of inflatable dolls. It subtly drove home the need to seat customers at a distance but was also whimsical rather than dictatorial in how they enforced the policy. The result brought energy into a reduced capacity environment.

Entrepreneur A experienced some serious setbacks not long after acquiring his business advisory services company. Those setbacks and circumstances were largely beyond his control and the mindset that he and his business partner brought when dealing with those circumstances influenced the actions he took, and in moving from righteous indignation to acceptance he earned the respect of his executive level staff. The principles he adopted in the new culture he established energized the firm and united them in identifying the actions the firm could take and focus on thriving, not hiding.

Entrepreneur B has a track record of creating the value chain and energizing culture that has taken 30 businesses from startup through funding and selling the business to the next level owners. In a business environment where four out of five businesses fail, it is no small accomplishment to be able to have that level of influence to guide businesses that focus on healthcare and learning. This does not even include the adjunct professor and local government advisory role.

Empower highlights

What is the legacy we want to create as business leaders? Here some options, define what your legacy is for you.

- being remembered as a key individual, which is instrumental in guiding a key company to success
- balancing our personal and professional calendars to avoid an either/or mindset and to protect the boundaries we set for our own definition of balance
- helping others to thrive growth and knowing our role in making that happen

The option is ours and the actions we take are a consequence of those choices.

Entrepreneur A has built a platform as an influencer in setting up businesses not only to thrive, but to operate in a manner that frees the business owner from being single threaded in all decisions, actions, while continuing to grow and meet their expanded business targets. Using a variety of media and forums, he attracts a number of opportunities to develop the capabilities of small business owners to follow the course he has set for his approach and many businesses can attribute their increased success and/or their viability to the adoption of his recommendations. The under pinning to his approach is to empower your executive team to make decisions and retain your top talent.

Entrepreneur B has created a legacy in a less public, but still impactful way. He empowers entrepreneurs at every stage in the process to learn and apply the principals and, although not as well-known, exerts a powerful influence on business owners and reverses the odds of failure by guiding them through taking the actions required to build a successful business model.

Evolve highlights

Time does not stand still and as we noted earlier the universe has a pull on us as individuals toward growth. Just as the sun and the moon influence the oceans, we are drawn to grow, not remain stagnant. We can ignore that pull for a time because we are energy, just as the universe is energy, we experience longing, discontent, and "dis-ease" that shows up in a variety of ways such as boredom, stress, depression, anxiety, and other symptoms. We can turn to a doctor to address the symptoms or we can self-cure by looking inward at the root cause of that longing or discontent and see what actions will bring us into better alignment with our purpose, dreams, and vision.

Entrepreneur A has evolved from life experience, learning as he went and not settling for the mindset that he could not be successful without permission. Many times, we wait for permission, having a degree, having money, or having influence before we think we are ready to evolve and move to the next level. What if we remain curious and think to ourselves, if someone else has done it, it must be feasible so I can do it too? What if we say to ourselves, even if we do not know anyone who has done it, maybe it is in my imagination because it is my purpose to be the pioneer and prove everyone else wrong? This is the mindset to continue to evolve over the course of our professional career or lifetime. This is the essence of Darwin's theory of evolution put into the context of what it means to our lives and our success.

Entrepreneur B has also evolved. Although he experienced immediate success with his first venture, he learned some lessons and applied those lessons to what he teaches and guides as he applies each new learning to the subsequent entrepreneurial and business advisory role he assumed. He had the financial wherewithal after the first success to just play. Yet, he made the decision to evolve, grow, and invest in the success of others. This has impacted the lives of countless individuals and his community at large. The ripple effects from this evolution can be seen in the companies he has influenced.

Evoke highlights

We do not travel down the path to success as business owners and leaders alone. It may seem lonely at times, if we are carving out a new path, yet we have the power to take the actions required to create a system of support. Explorers from the past are well-known, yet a single individual did not sail the ship or hack a path out of dense woods alone. They were the leader of the effort and gained the influence, but their influence was extended by evoking support from their crew.

Entrepreneur A deals with business owners every day whose longing and discontent revolves around their belief that they are slaves to their business and the business has overtaken some or all of the other dimensions of their lives. They make daily decisions not to eat healthy foods, not to exercise, not to spend time with their family, not to take time off under the belief that when the individual is the business, they don't have permission to define boundaries and processes that create the space on their calendar for these actions. His work is to open their perspectives and see that by creating the support in our business model and family models we can elevate above the current limiting belief that it can't be done and see a path, however tiny, and take the actions to make that path more well-worn and navigable to find a way to be successful and take time off and enjoy the benefits of running a thriving enterprise.

Entrepreneur B has a talent for evoking greatness in others. His insights and track record have cultivated a mindset for sharing the path to success and helping others build a roadmap to success. This does not mean that the companies did not ford some rivers, climb some mountains, or find and oasis in the desert easily, it means that he also evoked the mindset and actions to stay the course, do the actions even when we did not see a light at the end of a tunnel. This mentoring type relationship is one that we all should cultivate. We can use our mentor as a navigator and soundboard when we are weighed down by circumstances and cannot seem to see more than a win/lose set of options. They can ask us key questions that help us to evoke our imagination, experience, and confidence to see more than just two options and select a reasonable course of actions on one of the new options we see in the distance.

Parting thoughts to explore

Our journeys on the path to success intersected at this juncture. My hope is that we will meet again. Unlike the Slinky, DNA has intersection points along its spiral path. I have laid out a path for cultivating a growth mindset and charting a roadmap for creating a value chain approach to proven business success. I hope that by following these paths, they will intersect again.

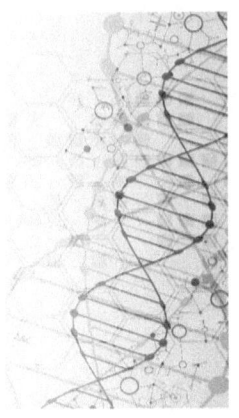

The stories and anecdotes in the book are meant to open our perspectives and see that there are different paths to success. Just like in a National or State Park with many trails, some end up at the spectacular waterfall and others end at the parking lot, when we do not even get out of the car because the path or trail seems too daunting. My hope is that when you find yourself in a circumstance or situation, and you do not just stay in the parking lot.

Maybe the next action is trying an easier path to build up endurance, another option is finding an experienced trail guide, or maybe it is setting a date on your calendar for a retry. There is not a marathon runner, mountain climber, or any other similar analogy that got it completely right the first time.

BIBLIOGRAPHY

1. "How the Slinky Sprang Into Stores 70 Years Ago". Time Inc. Retrieved 2018-01-03.
2. Dow, Sheila; Noce, Jaime E., eds. (2002). Business Leader Profiles for Students. 2. Detroit: Gale. pp. 238–241. ISBN 978-0-7876-6615-6.
3. Hunter, Ron; Waddell, Michael E. (2008). Toy Box Leadership: Leadership Lessons from the Toys We Loved as a Child.
4. Jump up to: [a b c d] "Inventor of the Week: The Slinky". MIT School of Engineering. Archived from the original on 2009-02-22. Retrieved 2009-02-24.
5. Jump up to: [a b c d e f g h i j k] Walsh, Tim (2005). Timeless Toys: Classic Toys and the Playmakers Who Created Them. Andrews McMeel Publishing. pp. 62–65. ISBN 978-0-7407-5571-2.
6. Przybys, John (March 1, 1998). "Novel Ideas". Las Vegas Review-Journal. Retrieved 2010-02-04.
7. Barnes, Julian E. (2001-01-28). "A Name, a Name, Destined for Fame". The New York Times. Retrieved 2009-02-26.
8. Jump up to: [a b c d e] Rich, Mark (2005). Warman's 101 Greatest Baby Boomer Toys. Iola, Wisconsin: KP Books. pp. 58–59. ISBN 0-89689-220-4.
9. "'Slinky' brainchild". Delaware County Daily Times. Retrieved 2014-01-25.
10. "Betty James, who cofounded Slinky company, dies". KXMB-TV. Associated Press. 2008-11-22. Retrieved 2009-02-25.
11. Jump up to: [a b c d] Hevesi, Dennis (2008-11-25). "Betty James, Who Named the Slinky Toy, Is Dead at 90". The New York Times. Retrieved 2009-02-25.
12. Ikenson, Ben. Patents: Ingenious Inventions: How They Work and How They Came to Be.
13. *Slinky drop physics - video of extended Slinky being dropped*. Discover magazine. 26 September 2011.

14. *Cross, Rod C.; Wheatland, Mike S. (22 Aug 2012). "Modeling a falling slinky". American Journal of Physics. **80** (12): 1051. arXiv:1208.4629. Bibcode:2012AmJPh..80.1051C. doi:10.1119/1.4750489.*
15. *Cross, Rod C.; Wheatland, Mike S. (2012). "Modeling a falling slinky". American Journal of Physics. American Association of Physics Teachers. **80** (12): 1051. arXiv:1208.4629. Bibcode:2012AmJPh..80.1051C. doi:10.1119/1.4750489.*
16. McDowell, Edwin (1998-11-28). "Helen H. Malsed, 88, Creator of Slinky Toys". *The New York Times*. Retrieved 2009-02-26.
    1. Witchel, Alex (1996-02-21). "Talking Toys with Betty James; Persevering for Family and Slinky". *The New York Times*. Retrieved 2009-02-26.
17. US patent 4120929, Reum, Donald James, "Method for producing a spirally wound plastic article", issued 17 October 1978
18. *Sourcebook for Receptive and Expressive Language*. Detroit, Michigan: Wayne State University Press. 2006. p. 106. ISBN 0-8143-3314-1. Retrieved 2009-02-25.
19. "Regular Session 2001–2002, House Bill 1893". Pennsylvania General Assembly. Retrieved 31 March 2011.
20. "Toy Industry Association Announces Its Century of Toys List" *(Press release)*. Business Wire for Toy Industry Association. 2003-01-21. Retrieved 2009-02-19.
21. Vanderbei, R. J. (2017). The Falling Slinky. *American Mathematical Monthly*, 124(1), 24. Retrieved 6 21, 2019, from https://maa.tandfonline.com/doi/abs/10.4169/amer.math.monthly.124.1.24
22. **https://www.insidescience.org/news/secrets-levitating-slinky**
23. Wikipedia 2019 HYPERLINK "https://hbr.org/2018/09/curiosity" \l "the-five-dimensions-of-curiosity" https://hbr.org/2018/09/curiosity#the-five-dimensions-of-curiosity
    - HYPERLINK "https://hbr.org/search?term=todd%20b.%20kashdan" Todd B. Kashdan
    - HYPERLINK "https://hbr.org/search?term=david%20j.%20disabato" David J. Disabato
    - HYPERLINK "https://hbr.org/search?term=fallon%20r.%20goodman" Fallon R. Goodman
    - HYPERLINK "https://hbr.org/search?term=carl%20naughton" Carl Naughton
24. HYPERLINK "https://davidcummings.org" https://davidcummings.org

www.ingramcontent.com/pod-product-compliance
Lightning Source LLC
Chambersburg PA
CBHW020740180526
45163CB00001B/296